Summer Bridge Activities™ 7-8

Created by   Michele D. Van Leeuwen

Written by   Dr. Leland Graham
Darriell Ledbetter
Frankie Long

Summer Bridge Activities™ 7–8

For information, write:
Rainbow Bridge Publishing
PO Box 571470
Salt Lake City, UT 84157-1470
801-268-8887

www.summerbridgeactivities.com

www.summerbrains.com

Publisher
Scott G. Van Leeuwen

Associate Publisher
George Starks

Product Development Director
Dante J. Orazzi

Copy Editors and Proofreaders
Kim Carlson, Melody Feist, Jeanna Mason, Paul Rawlins

Graphic Design and Layout
Andy Carlson, Robyn Funk, Zack Johnson

Cover Art
Bryan Beach

Printing History:
First Printing 1998
Second Printing 1999
Third Printing 2000
Fourth Printing 2001
Fifth Printing 2002
Sixth Printing 2003

ISBN: 1-887923-10-1

Printed in the United States of America
10 9 8 7 6

Table of Contents

Creating Partnerships...iv

Summer Bridge Activities™ Blueprint for Success...v

Social Skills and Self-Worth vii

How to Maximize Summer Bridge Activities™ ix

Encourage Your Child to Read..x

Reading Book List xi

1st Section

    Incentive Contract Calendar 1

    My Plans for the Summer 2

    15 Daily Activities in Math, Reading, Writing, and Language.....................3

2nd Section

    Incentive Contract Calendar 33

    My Best Day/Vacation So Far 34

    20 Daily Activities in Math, Reading, Writing, and Language...................35

3rd Section

    Incentive Contract Calendar 75

    Get Ready for Back to School 76

    15 Daily Activities in Math, Reading, Writing, and Language...................77

Answer Pages...107

Reference Pages 114

Building Better Bodies and Behavior..127

Creating Partnerships

Dear Parents,

Welcome to Summer Bridge Activities™! You're creating a partnership because you've become involved in your child's education. Picking up this workbook clearly shows your child that education is important, something to value.

Let me tell you how this unique series of workbooks came to be. As a parent with school age children, and with the summer quickly approaching, I was concerned the skills they had worked so hard to develop would take a good licking if I didn't do something to support them. In addition, I was apprehensive about their adjustment to school in the fall after three months of playing.

I went to their teachers for help. In speaking with them, other school administrators, and parents, I found I wasn't alone with my concerns. In fact, I was told approximately 80 percent of what children are taught in school is lost within a month, unless that knowledge is reinforced quickly and continuously! I certainly didn't want that to happen to my children.

The search began. I looked all over for appropriate workbooks. I'm sure you'll agree, if you've ever gone out looking, there are lots to choose from. But they're either too hard or too simple or didn't match what my children learned in school. I wasn't looking for perfection, but it sure seemed that way. I simply wanted to buy something that correlated with the curriculum guidelines from the department of education.

I found myself back in front of my children's teachers, asking where I could find such materials. They knew of none. So…

With a team composed of award-winning teachers, informed educators, and concerned parents, we put our own books together. You have in your hands the results of literally thousands of hours of work. All of the activities—over 100 in each book—follow the curriculum guidelines I mentioned earlier. And we've taken it one step further—Summer Bridge Activities™ has been successfully tested on thousands of children.

And what about my children—or better yet, what about your children? If you'd like to find them
- thinking while having fun,
- motivated by a desire to learn,
- confident and excited when the new school year rolls around …

And if you'd like to
- reach your goal of keeping your child active the smart way,
- successfully bridge the gap over the summer
- with an easy-to-use daily program—
- all without hassles—
- yet, produce the results of busy, happy, and learning children, it can now be accomplished.

Use Summer Bridge Activities™ as suggested. We've got many testimonials to the workbooks' successes.

It's terrific that you're involved. Thank you for your purchase. We at RBP Books would love to hear about your success. Call 1-800-598-1441 with your story.

Best to you,

Michele D. Van Leeuwen

Michele D. Van Leeuwen
Creator of Summer Bridge Activities™

P.S.: Summer Bridge Activities™, preschool through 8th grade, also work great for those students who are off-track from year-round school, vacations, trips, illness, breaks from school, etc. Try it.

Summer Bridge Activities™ Blueprint for Success

Books You'll Love to Read

- A suggested list of reading books (xi).
- The recommended time for reading each day is 1 to 1 1/2 hours. This amount of time will help your child maintain and increase reading skills.
- It is suggested that you determine the amount of reading time that is best for you. By reading every day your child will find success in future challenges.
- Set a goal to develop good reading habits.

SBA Incentive Contract Calendars

- Calendars are located at the beginning of each section.
- We suggest that the parent and child sign the SBA Incentive Contract Calendar before the child begins each section.
- When your child completes one day of Summer Bridge Activities™, he/she checks the appropriate box.
- Refer to the recommended reading times. When your child completes the agreed reading time each day, he/she checks the appropriate box.
- The parent may initial the SBA Incentive Contract Calendar once the activities have been completed.

Sections of Summer Bridge Activities™

- There are three sections in Summer Bridge Activities™; the first and second review, the third previews.
- Each section begins with an SBA Incentive Contract Calendar.™
- Each section covers four subjects:
    Language Arts, Mathematics, Social Studies, Science
- Each day your child will complete activities in two of the four subjects.
- Each section becomes progressively more challenging.

Language Arts
7th grade in Review
- Parts of Speech • Punctuation • Reading Comprehension • Agreement
- Complements • Diagramming • Clauses • Run-On Sentences and Fragments
- Writing • Paragraphs and Essays

8th grade in Preview
- Verbs • Nouns • Pronouns • Clauses • Context Clues • Homophones • Possessives
- Run-On Sentences • Fragments • Subjects • Predicates • Comparisons

Mathematics
7th grade in Review
- Estimation • Integers • Geometry • Equations • Graphing • Statistics
- Probability

8th grade in Preview
- Integers • Expressions • Equations • Polynomials • Rational Numbers • Exponents
- Square Roots

Social Studies
7th grade in Review
- Physical and Cultural Geography • Economics • Charts • Graphs • Maps • Tables

8th grade in Preview
- Physical Geography • Charts • Maps • Cultural Geography • History • Timeline

Science
7th grade in Review
- Life Science • Earth Science • Physical Science

8th grade in Preview
- Body Systems • Solar System • Heredity • Energy

This section includes some fun experiments, but they can also be dangerous, so remember: **Safety First!** Be sure your work area is clean and safe. Use aprons to protect your clothing. Use safety glasses when necessary. Follow directions carefully. Label all containers. Even after all that, our attorney insisted that we stress the importance of safety by providing you with the following warning:

The science experiments presented in this book should only be performed under adult supervision. Failure to follow the precise instructions in the text may result in bodily injury, property damage or death. The author and publisher cannot be responsible for any injuries or property damage received as a result of deviation from the text or failure to provide adequate adult supervision.

Social Skills and Self-Worth

Be Honest with Yourself and Other People. Realize that honesty is the only way these social skills will work. Dishonesty may work for a little while, but it will catch up with you and soon be discovered. Your integrity is vital to your self-worth. Value yourself and others will.

Have Pride in Yourself. There is no point in trying to be different from who you really are. Others will find out what you are like anyway. There may be things you want to improve on to become a better person, but be proud of who you are. No one likes a phony.

Stay True to Your Principles. Don't give up what you believe in to make friends. Think about what you believe in, be confident in yourself, and know why you believe this way. You do not have to change in order for anyone to like you.

Lend a Listening Ear. Listening to others makes them feel good and important. Look them in the eyes. Give them your full attention. By listening, you compliment them, and they will like you for that.

Seek Common Ground. The places you go determine the kind of people you will meet. Get out and mix with others. Introduce yourself. Keep in mind most people are just as cautious as you are about meeting people. Generally, they will be glad you spoke first.

Dress to Impress. When you go out, others will notice your general appearance before you even have a chance to speak. Take pride in yourself and how you look.

Remembering Names & Faces. Follow these three simple steps:
   a. Hear the name so you can remember it. If you were unable to catch their name the first time, ask again – that is a compliment. It shows that you are interested.
   b. In your conversation, call them by their name as soon as possible. This will help you remember.
   c. Picture their name spelled out in your mind, with their face in the background, or relate their name with something familiar to help you remember.

Talk with Confidence in Your Voice. When you use your voice, be kind, clear and enthusiastic. Avoid being a loud mouth, and include others in conversation. You will make friends by making others feel part of the activity.

Have Personality. Smile, you will win friends. Have humor, everyone needs to laugh. Friendship is all about having fun!

Lend a Helping Hand. You'll be admired for your kindness. Politeness shows respect for others.

Initiate a Conversation. Talk about famous people, your favorite athletes, or current events.

Keep the Conversation Alive. Find out what the other person's interests are. Ask questions like: "What do you like doing after school?" "Where were you born?" "What is your favorite movie?" These types of questions require more than just "yes" or "no" answers. Listen to the response. Look for things that both of you have a common interest in to keep the conversation alive.

Everybody Has an Opinion. Share your opinions, but respect other people's right to have their own opinion, which may be different than yours.

Don't Burden Others. When trying to develop a friendship, keep your problems to yourself until a later time. Forcing your burdens on someone may scare them away.

Respect Privacy. Talk about common interests, but do not pry into their personal life.

Don't Be a Gossiper. When you gossip you hurt others as well as yourself. People who gossip lose the trust of others and may lose the chance to make new friends.

Confidence in Yourself. Share your accomplishments, but don't brag or boast (to praise yourself or your possessions). Nothing will turn someone away faster than bragging.

Be Positive with Your Friends. Build up your friends by complimenting them on their strengths instead of tearing them down in front of others. Everybody has weaknesses, including you. With a friend's support, weaknesses can become strengths. People like to be around others who make them feel good about themselves and the company they keep.

How to Maximize
Summer Bridge Activities™

 First, let your child explore the book. Flip through the pages and look at the activities with your child to help him/her become familiar with the book.

 Help select a good time for reading or working on the activities. Suggest a time before your child has played outside and becomes too tired to do the work.

 Provide any necessary materials.

 Offer positive guidance. Remember, the activities are not meant to be tests. You want to create a relaxed and positive attitude toward learning. Work through at least one example on each page with your child. "Think aloud" and show your child how to solve problems.

 Give your child plenty of time to think. You may be surprised by how much children can do on their own.

 Stretch your child's thinking beyond the page. If you are reading a book, you might ask, "What do you think will happen next?" or "What would you do if this happened to you?" Encourage your child to talk about their interests and observations about the world around them.

 Reread stories and occasionally flip through completed pages. Completed pages and books will be a source of pride to your child and will help show how much he/she accomplished over the summer.

 Read and work on activities while outside. Take the workbook out in the backyard, or a family campout. It can be fun wherever you are!

 Encourage siblings, relatives, and neighborhood friends to help with reading and activities. Other children are often perfect for providing the one-on-one attention necessary to reinforce reading skills.

 Give plenty of approval! Stickers and stamps, are effective for recognizing a job well done. At the end of the summer, your child can feel proud of his/her accomplishments and will be eager for school to start.

Encourage Your Child to Read

*R*eading is the primary means to all learning. If a child cannot read effectively, other classroom subjects can remain out of reach.

*Y*ou were probably the first person to introduce your child to the wonderful world of reading. As your child grows, it is important to continue encouraging his/her interest in reading to support the skills they are being taught in school.

*T*his summer, make reading a priority in your household. Set aside time each day to read. Encourage your child take a break from playing, and stretch out with a book found on the Summer Activities™ Reading Book List. Choose a title that you have never read, or introduce your child to some of the books you enjoyed when you were his/her age! Books only seem to get better with time!

*V*isit the library to find books that meet your child's specific interests. Ask a librarian which books are popular among children of your child's grade. Take advantage of summer activities at the library. Ask the librarian about other resources, such as stories on cassette, compact disc, and the Internet.

*E*ncourage reading in all settings and daily activities. Encourage your child to tell you about things he/she reads.

*B*est of all, show your child how much YOU like to read! Sit down with your child when he/she reads and enjoy a good book yourself. After dinner, share stories and ideas from newspapers and magazines that might interest your child. Make reading a way of life this summer!

Reading Book List

Aiken, Joan
Wolves of Willoughby Chase, The

Armstrong, William
Sounder

Babbitt, Natalie
Search for Delicious, The

Barron, T. A.
Ancient One, The

Birdseye, Tom
Tucker

Bond, Nancy
String in the Harp, A

Burch, Robert
Queenie Peavy

Burnett, Frances
Little Princess, A
Secret Garden, The

Burnford, Shelia
Incredible Journey, The

Calvert, Patricia
Snowbird, The

Choi, Sook Nyul
Year of Impossible Good-byes

Cleaver, Vera
Where the Lilies Bloom

Cooper, Susan
Grey King, The
Over Sea, Under Stone

Corcoran, Barbara
Sky Is Falling, The

Crew, Linda
Children of the River

Cushman, Karen
Catherine, Called Birdy

Dahl, Roald
James and the Giant Peach

Daugherty, James
Daniel Boone

DeAngeli, Maguerite
Door in the Wall, The

De Saint-Exupery, Antoine
Little Prince, The

DeTrevino, Elizabeth
I, Juan de Pareja

DuBois, William
Twenty-One Balloons, The

Eckert, Allan W.
Incident at Hawk's Hill

Edwards, Julie
Last of the Really Great
Whangdoodles

Enright, Elizabeth
Gone-Away Lake

Estes, Eleanor
Hundred Dresses, The

Field, Rachel
Hitty, Her First Hundred Years

Fitzgerald, John D.
Great Brain at the Academy,
The

Forbes, Esther
Johnny Tremain

Fox, Paula
Slave Dancer, The

Freedman, Russell
Wright Brothers . . . Airplane,
The

Gannett, Ruth S.
My Father's Dragon

Gray, Elizabeth J.
Adam of the Road

Guy, Rosa
Music of Summer, The

Hahn, Mary Downing
Spanish Kidnapping Disaster,
The

Heide, Florence
Banana Twist

Holm, Anne
North to Freedom

Hudson, Jan
Sweetgrass

Hunt, Irene
Across Five Aprils
Up a Road Slowly

James, Will
Smoky, the Cow Horse

Juster, Norton
Phantom Tollbooth, The

Keith, Harold
Rifles for Watie

Kelly, Eric P.
Trumpeter of Krakow, The

Kendall, Carol
Gammage Cup, The

Krumgold, Joseph
And Now Miguel

L'Engle, Madeleine
Ring of Endless Light, A

Langton, Jane
Fledgling, The

Lawson, Robert
Ben and Me
Rabbit Hill

LeGuin, Ursula K.
Tombs of Atuan, The

Lewis, Elizabeth
Young Fu of the Upper
Yangtze

Lindbergh, Anne
Travel Far, Pay No Fare

Lindgren, Astrid
Pippi Longstocking

Lofting, Hugh
Voyages of Doctor Dolittle,
The

London, Jack
Call of the Wild, The
White Fang

Lowry, Lois
Anastasia at Your Service
Taking Care of Terrific

Lyons, Mary E.
Letters from a Slave Girl

MacDonald, Betty
Hello, Mrs. Piggle-Wiggle

McKinley, Robin
Blue Sword, The
Hero and the Crown, The

Meigs, Cornelia
Willow Whistle, The

Merrill, Jean
Pushcart War, The

Montgomery, L.M.
Anne of Green Gables

Naidoo, Beverley
Chain of Fire

Huynh, Quang Nhuong
Land I Lost, The

North, Sterling
Rascal

Paterson, Katherine
Bridge to Terabithia
Jacob Have I Loved

Pullman, Philip
Detective Stories

Reeder, Carolyn
Foster's War

Richter, Conrad
Light in the Forest, The

Roberts, Willo D.
Baby-Sitting Is a Dangerous Job

Rottman, S. L.
Rough Waters

Ruckman, Ivy
Night of the Twisters

Seredy, Kate
White Stag, The

Sewell, Anna
Black Beauty

Sidney, Margaret
Five Little Peppers and How
They Grew

Smith, Roland
Sasquatch

Snyder, Zilpha K.
Headless Cupid, The
Witches of Worm, The

Stevermer, Caroline
River Rats

Taylor, Mildred
Let the Circle Be Unbroken
Roll of Thunder, Hear My Cry

Taylor, Theodore
Cay, The

Temple, Frances
Taste of Salt

Thesman, Jean
When the Road Ends

Travers, P.L.
Mary Poppins

Walsh, Jill Paton
Green Book, The

Yep, Laurence
Dragonwings

Zindel, Paul
Pigman and Me, The
Reef of Death

Incentive Contract Calendar

Month _____

My parents and I decided that if I complete 15 days of
Summer Bridge Activities™ 7–8 and read _____ minutes a day,
my incentive/reward will be:

_____

Child's Signature_____

Parent's Signature_____

EXAMPLE: ☑ ☑ _AC_

Day 1 ☐ ☐ _____

Day 2 ☐ ☐ _____

Day 3 ☐ ☐ _____

Day 4 ☐ ☐ _____

Day 5 ☐ ☐ _____

Day 6 ☐ ☐ _____

Day 7 ☐ ☐ _____

Day 8 ☐ ☐ _____

Day 9 ☐ ☐ _____

Day 10 ☐ ☐ _____

Day 11 ☐ ☐ _____

Day 12 ☐ ☐ _____

Day 13 ☐ ☐ _____

Day 14 ☐ ☐ _____

Day 15 ☐ ☐ _____

Child: Put a ✔ in the ☐ for the daily activities ☐ completed.

Put a ✔ in the ☐ for the daily reading 📘 completed.

Parent: Initial the _____ for daily activities and reading your child completes.

My plans for the Summer!

What I want to do...

Where I want to go...

What I want to see...

People I want to hang out with...

What I want to learn...

2

Sentence Types. On the line following each sentence, identify each sentence as *imperative*, *interrogative*, *declarative*, or *exclamatory*.

Need Help? Check Out Grammar Links at www.summerbrains.com

1. What are you planning to do this summer on vacation? _____

2. Jennifer and Mark were at the library when their package came. _____

3. Do the two red apples on the desk belong to Josh or Sarieke? _____

4. Why are you going? _____

5. The ancient Romans sometimes gave people second names. _____

6. Walking to school, William was splashed by a passing car. _____

7. Fridays and other days with tests have always seemed to be longer. _____

8. My old bicycle with the uncomfortable seat is rusting in Dan's garage. _____

9. Give me the dustcloth, and I will help you. _____

A *descriptive paragraph* is one that tells what something is like or what it looks like. In developing a descriptive paragraph, describe parts of a person, place, or thing. Use mostly sensory details to tell what you see, hear, smell, taste, or touch. For example, what does a rattlesnake look like? Or what kind of sound does a rock make when it is dropped into a pool of water? Or what does a new shirt or blouse smell like? Write a paragraph in which you describe someone you know, a place you have visited, or a thing that interests you.

_____

_____

_____

_____

_____

_____

_____

_____

_____

_____

_____

_____

_____

_____

Add, subtract, multiply, or divide.

1. 234.8 – 27.9	2. 45.876 + 9.05	3. 43.27 x 1.68	4. 67.904 – 3.628	5. 760.32 + 94.09

6. 45.3 ÷ 3 = _____

7. 78.2 ÷ 2 = _____

8. 125.5 ÷ 5 = _____

9. 2(5 + 8) = _____

10. (7 + 9) ÷ (4 x 2) = _____

11. 8(21 – 9) = _____

Solve the following problems using the necessary operations.

12. Sally has 24 pictures from her trip. Her photo album has 8 pages. If she puts the same number of pictures on each page, how many pictures will be on each page?

13. Jason wants to go to a baseball game and take a rafting trip. If he has $49.00 and spends $26.00 at the ball game, what does he have left to use for the rafting trip?

14. Meg saves old newspapers for her neighborhood to recycle. On Monday she has gathered 75 pounds of newspapers. The recycling center pays 9¢ per pound for newspapers. How much will she get for her Monday collection?

15. A store is having a sale on running shoes. James wants a pair that costs $49.00. He also wants to purchase 3 pairs of socks that cost $2.95 each. How much will the socks and shoes cost altogether?

16. Chelsea and her mother like to go to the movies. If they go to a matinee, the price is less than an evening show. In March they attended 12 matinees and 4 evening shows. All matinee tickets cost $3.50 per ticket. The evening shows are $4.00 for a child's ticket and $6.00 for an adult ticket. How much did they spend on movie tickets in March?

Geographic Features. The crossword puzzle below is composed of terms common to physical geography. Each definition describes only one term correctly.

Word Bank
steppes
tributary
savanna
fjord
mesa
strait
reef
isthmus
butte
pampas
dune
oasis
delta
canyon
cape
lagoon
plateau
veld
reservoir
glacier

Across

2. a narrow piece of land that projects into a body of water

4. large, slow-moving sheet of ice

5. roughly triangular land at the mouth of a river formed from deposits of silt

8. water partially or completely enclosed within an atoll

9. semi-dry plains with sparse vegetation

12. fertile area in a desert with a steady water supply

13. broad, grassy plains in South Africa

14. Spanish for *table*; steep-sided, flat-topped land

16. small, flat-topped hill

17. narrow body of water connecting two larger bodies of water

19. inlet of the sea between high, steep cliffs

Down

1. natural or man-made water-holding site

3. Argentina's vast, grassy plains

5. a sandy hill formed by the wind

6. steep-sided, narrow, deep valley

7. large, high, flat area that rises above the surrounding land

10. smaller river or stream that flows into a larger one

11. flat, open grassland with scattered trees and shrubs

15. narrow strip of land connecting two larger land masses

18. sand, rock, or coral ridge at or near the surface of the water

Changing Surface of the Earth. The surface, or crust, of the earth is constantly changing. Mountains and valleys that exist today probably looked quite different millions of years ago. Our oceans today may have been mountains and valleys a long time ago. There are actually movements taking place constantly on the earth's surface, some too small and too slow to be directly noticed. What causes these movements in the earth's crust? What will the earth's surface look like in another million years?

Fill in the blanks using the Word Bank provided.

Word Bank
fault
plateau
fracture
hanging wall
crust
normal fault
stress
tension
lateral fault

1. The outermost layer, or surface, of the earth is called the _____.
2. A crack in a rock is called a _____.
3. _____ pushes and pulls on the earth's crust.
4. A break or crack along which rocks move is called a _____.
5. _____ is stress that pulls on rocks of the crust.
6. In a _____, the hanging wall moves down relative to the foot wall.
7. In a _____, blocks of rock slide horizontally past each other.
8. A _____ is a large area of flat land that is raised high above sea level.
9. A block of rock above a fault is called the _____.

True or False.
Decide whether each statement below is true or false. Write T for true. If false, write F, and then change the underlined word or words to make the statement true.

____10. Molten rock found beneath the earth's surface is called <u>lava</u>. _____

____11. Mountains formed by blocks of rock uplifted by normal faults are called <u>dome mountains</u>. _____

____12. The outermost layer of the earth is called the <u>mantle</u>. _____

____13. The squeezing together of rocks by stress is called <u>compression</u>. _____

____14. An upward fold is called an <u>anticline</u>. _____

Time Out: Write a brief paragraph in which you describe two ways in which plateaus can be formed. Can you describe how the shape of a plateau differs from that of a mountain?

_____

_____

_____

_____

A *sentence fragment* is a group of words that is only part of a sentence. It does not have both a subject and a predicate, and it does not express a complete thought. A *run-on* sentence is two or more sentences run together without correct punctuation. In the following, indicate whether each group of words is a sentence, fragment, or run-on.

1. One of the greatest men in the twentieth century was Martin Luther King, Jr., he was responsible for the Civil Rights law. _____

2. Running down the hall with all the books he could carry. _____

3. I was there when he prepared to give his greatest speech of all. _____

4. If everyone will get there on time after the last bell rings on Friday. _____

5. I am going to the grocery store on the corner beside the video store, does anyone need anything? _____

6. After he came back from Paris, his mother talked to him about his favorite places and food the neighbors wanted to know the same things. _____

A *phrase* is a group of words that does not contain a subject and a verb. In the following sentences, identify each phrase in bold print as a *prepositional phrase, infinitive phrase, participial phrase, gerund phrase,* or *appositive phrase.*

neeD Help?
Check Out
Grammar Links at
www.summerbrains.com

7. At the football game, people wanted to stand **in their seats.** _____

8. The student player **jumping like a calf in the pasture** was fun to watch. _____

9. **Swimming in the summertime** is my favorite pastime. _____

10. When we went **to Oregon**, we saw many beautiful forests. _____

11. Mrs. Murray, **my conscientious and wonderful teacher**, is my hero. _____

12. On their way home from vacation, the neighbors saw a strange-looking animal, **something with long legs, a long neck, and lots of fur on its body.** _____

13. **To be or not to be** is the question. _____

14. Did Josh and Jim enjoy **camping in the park** this past weekend? _____

15. After a short time, we heard the dog **barking crazily at the cat.** _____

Multiplication and Division with Decimals. Round division problems to the nearest hundredth.

1. 4.67) 87.9

2. 34.6) 65.32

3. 58.1) 987.3

4. 678.45
    x 3.26

5. 34.670
    x 4.8

6. 560.02
    x 76.34

7. .345) 7.321

8. 2.309) 8.956

9. 7.3) 56.98

Set up each of the following problems in the correct form and solve.

10. David bought 15 gallons of gasoline. His total cost was $13.60. How much was the gasoline per gallon?

11. Sam saw a cactus on his vacation that was 12.4 times as tall as he was. If Sam is 42 inches tall, how tall was the cactus?

12. It took Janice two hours to drive 23.5 miles in heavy traffic. What was her average speed in miles per hour?

13. Denise began painting birdhouses to sell. If she paints 12.8 birdhouses in one week, how many will she be able to paint in fifteen weeks?

North America Map. Label the numbered countries, rivers, and oceans. Label the countries' capitals. Put a star where you live. Consult an atlas for assistance.

North America

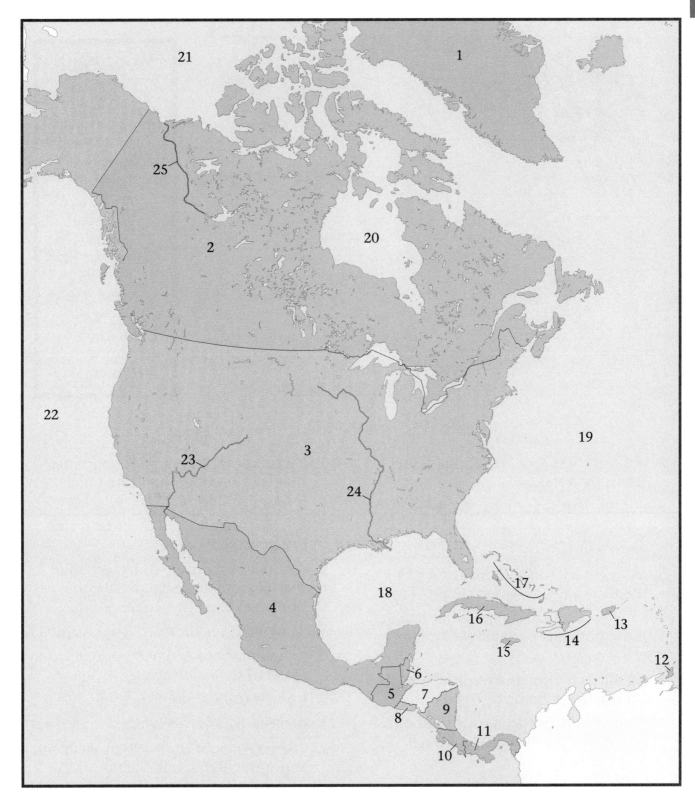

Rocks and Minerals. Rocks are the building blocks of the earth. Rocks form mountains, ocean floors, beaches, and other parts of the earth's surface. Rocks have been used as building blocks *on* the earth in such places as Stonehenge and the pyramids. What is a rock? In science, a rock is a hard substance composed of one or more minerals or mineral-like substances. What is a mineral? A mineral is a naturally occurring, inorganic solid that has a definite chemical composition and crystalline structure. Silver is a mineral; steel is not. Silver occurs naturally, and steel is man-made.

Use the Word Bank to complete the crossword puzzle.

Word Bank
chemical
clastic
conglomerate
extrusive
gemstone
igneous
inorganic
intrusive
metal
metamorphic
mineral
nonmetal
ore
organic
rock
sedimentary

Need Help?
Check Out
Science Links at
www.summerbrains.com

Across

2. smooth rocks that have been worn down by water

5. not formed from living things

6. igneous rock formed from lava on the earth's surface

8. sedimentary rock formed from fragments of previously existing rocks

10. a hard substance composed of one or more minerals or mineral-like substances

11. changed in form as a result of chemical reactions, pressure, or heat

13. formed from particles carried along and deposited by wind and water

Down

1. a hard, beautiful, durable substance that can be cut and polished for jewelry and decoration

3. element that has a dull surface; not easily shaped

4. naturally occurring, inorganic solid that has a definite chemical composition and crystalline shape

5. an igneous rock formed from magma

7. sedimentary rock that is formed from material that was once alive

9. formed from molten rock

11. element that conducts electricity and heat

12. mineral or rock from which metals and nonmetals can be removed in usable amounts

A *direct object* answers the questions *what?* or *whom?* after an action verb. An *indirect object* answers the questions *to what?* (whom?) or *for what?* (whom?) after an action verb. In the following sentences, identify any direct (d.o.) and/or indirect objects (i.o.) on the lines provided.

1. Princess Diana gave much time to help various charities. _____

2. The teacher helped Jennifer do the homework after school. _____

3. Mother baked my sister a big chocolate cake for her birthday. _____

4. The divers swam freely through the crystal clear waters of the gulf. _____

5. Enormous colorful sails propelled the fast ships quickly over the seas. _____

6. The big ships brought merchants goods from all over the world. _____

7. Other English teachers took their students and their friends to the play. _____

8. Over the intercom, the principal gave the students a guarantee of honesty. _____

9. Walking home in the rain, Chris became very wet and cold and finally sick. _____

10. Why did you give the puppy so much puppy food? _____

An *adjective* is a word that describes a noun or pronoun. An *adverb* is a word that describes a verb, adjective, or another adverb. In the following sentences, draw a circle around each adjective (other than *a*, *an*, *the*) and an X over each adverb.

11. The great playwright was born in Stratford-on-Avon, England, in 1564.

12. These snow-covered mountains are part of the frequently visited Appalachian Mountains.

13. I watched the spectacular opening ceremonies of the Olympic Games in the city of Atlanta.

14. Quickly, the students hurried to their empty desks as the teacher walked down the hall.

15. The brightly burning candle amazed everyone at the very big birthday party.

16. Seven students worked carefully and wisely before they decided to ask for help.

17. After walking through the thick, dark woods for four hours, we decided to rest quietly.

18. Fonda gave much thought to her decision today before she decided to leave town proudly.

19. The twins were sick and hungry.

20. Everyone at the airport was waiting anxiously for the proud school winners to arrive.

Multiplying Fractions.

Multiplying fractions is similar to adding fractions. However, you multiply both the numerators and the denominators. It is not necessary to have common denominators.

Example: $\frac{2}{3} \times \frac{1}{3} = \frac{2}{9}$ and $\frac{1}{5} \times \frac{2}{3} = \frac{2}{15}$ Always be sure your answer is in simplest form.

1. $\frac{4}{7} \times \frac{2}{7} =$ 2. $\frac{3}{8} \times \frac{5}{8} =$ 3. $\frac{3}{9} \times \frac{8}{9} =$ 4. $\frac{9}{15} \times \frac{2}{3} =$ 5. $\frac{1}{5} \times \frac{2}{3} =$

6. $\frac{2}{3} \times \frac{6}{10} =$ 7. $\frac{7}{10} \times \frac{2}{3} =$ 8. $\frac{2}{5} \times \frac{5}{8} =$ 9. $\frac{5}{6} \times \frac{1}{3} =$ 10. $\frac{3}{7} \times \frac{4}{5} =$

11. $\frac{5}{8} \times \frac{1}{2} =$ 12. $\frac{1}{3} \times \frac{5}{8} =$ 13. $\frac{7}{9} \times \frac{4}{5} =$ 14. $\frac{9}{10} \times \frac{2}{3} =$ 15. $\frac{2}{9} \times \frac{7}{11} =$

Keep in mind that when you multiply fractions, your product will be a smaller number. Think about it! $2 \times \frac{1}{2} = 1$

Using what you know, solve the following word problems.

16. One half of Grayson's garden is used for vegetables. Of the remaining $\frac{1}{2}$, $\frac{2}{3}$ is used for flowers. What part of the garden is used for flowers?

17. If you and your friends eat half of a $\frac{3}{4}$ pound bag of candy, what part of a pound of candy have you eaten?

18. John has $\frac{4}{5}$ of the pages in his project done. He completed $\frac{2}{9}$ of those pages the first day he started. How many pages did he do the first day?

Caribbean Map. Label the major bodies of water, major countries, their capitals, and major islands. Use an orange pencil to trace the Tropic of Cancer. Consult a world atlas for assistance.

Caribbean

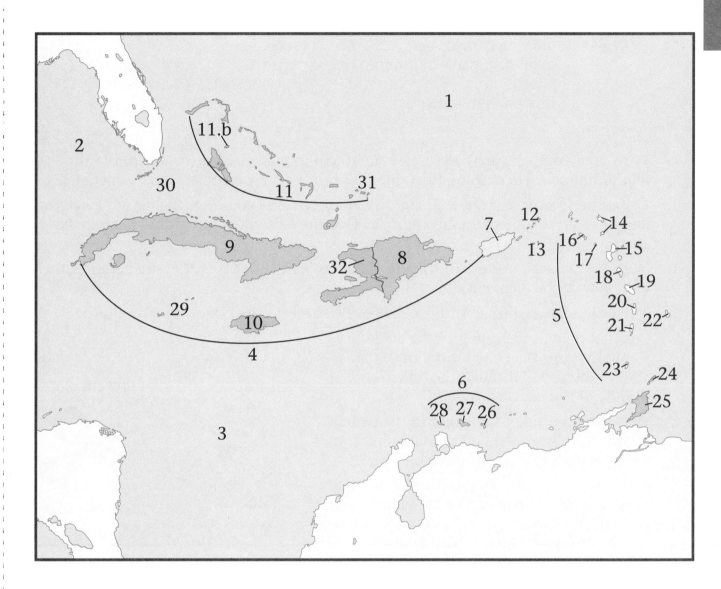

Erosion. A major source of erosion and deposition is running water, which picks up and wears away materials as it flows over the land. Water carries dissolved minerals and particles of mud. On rare occasions, running water can even sweep away large objects such as hillsides, boulders, and houses. Running water has a great deal of energy. In this next experiment, you will notice how this energy can be harnessed and put to work for humans.

Materials:

drawing compass	ruler
small disposable aluminum pan	scissors
pencil	piece of string 45 cm long
small weight (eraser)	

Procedure:

1. With your compass, draw a circle about 10 cm in diameter on the bottom of the aluminum pan. Then, using the same center hole, draw a circle 3 cm in diameter.

2. Using the scissors, cut out a 10 cm disk along the line you drew in step 1. *Do not cut along the line you drew for the 3 cm circle.* **Careful:** The cut edges of the pan may be sharp.

3. With the scissors, make eight cuts in the disk. Start the cuts at the outer edge of the disc; stop at the 3 cm circle.

4. Twist each part a quarter-turn clockwise. **Be careful. The edges may be sharp.**

5. Punch a hole in the center of the circle. Carefully push the pencil through the hole, sliding the pencil through the hole to the middle of the pencil.

6. Connect one end of the string to the pencil (about 3 cm from the circle). Make sure the string is tight around the pencil.

7. Connect the other end of the string to the weight. Now use one end of the pencil to hold the disk under the water faucet with a steady stream of water. What happened?

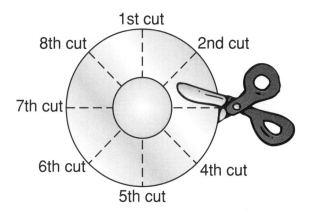

Follow Up: What is the connection between the water wheel (disk) and erosion? In your discussion, mention the role water and energy play in erosion.

_____

_____

_____

_____

_____

_____

Subject complements complete the meaning of a linking verb and identify or describe the subject. One complement is a *predicate nominative,* which is a noun or pronoun that follows a linking verb and identifies the subject. Another complement is a *predicate adjective,* which is an adjective that follows a linking verb and describes the subject. In the following sentences, indicate on the lines provided if there are any predicate nominatives (p.n.) or predicate adjectives (p.a.).

Need Help?
Check Out
Grammar Links at
www.summerbrains.com

1. A nuclear power plant leak can be very dangerous. _____

2. This piece of ground looks very swampy. _____

3. Priscilla Click is class president of her junior class. _____

4. The grand prize was a brand new Ford car from the store. _____

5. William Shakespeare was a great playwright from England. _____

6. Before becoming class secretary, Josh was the soccer team captain. _____

7. Written in the nineteenth century, *Walden* is still a great book. _____

8. Lemonade tastes cool on a hot day. _____

9. He is Tanner. _____

10. The art at the Huntsville Museum of Art is quite impressive. _____

An *evaluation paragraph* is one in which you decide on the value of an item or make a judgment about its importance. For example, did you enjoy the last movie you saw? Did you enjoy the last story you read? Did you enjoy the last book you read? Would you recommend these selections to your friends? Why or why not? In writing a paragraph to answer these questions, you would be writing an *evaluation paragraph.* This involves a process of deciding if something is good or bad. Write a paragraph below in which you evaluate the last movie you saw or the last story or book you read. Make sure you support or give reasons for your opinions.

_____

_____

_____

_____

_____

_____

_____

_____

_____

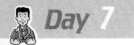
Adding and Subtracting Mixed Numbers.

When adding and subtracting mixed numbers, you also need to add or subtract the whole numbers. Always check to see if the answer is in simplest form. (<u>Hint</u>: Sometimes in subtraction it may be necessary to borrow from the whole number to increase the fraction in order to solve the problem.)

Reduce these fractions to simplest form.

1. $\frac{28}{5}$ = —   2. $\frac{37}{5}$ = —   3. $\frac{19}{7}$ = —   4. $\frac{41}{6}$ = —   5. $\frac{63}{8}$ = —

Change these fractions to have like denominators.

6. $\frac{5}{9}$ and $\frac{3}{11}$ 7. $\frac{4}{10}$ and $\frac{5}{8}$ 8. $\frac{7}{13}$ and $\frac{5}{7}$ 9. $\frac{3}{17}$ and $\frac{9}{14}$

Find the least common denominator for each set of fractions and add or subtract.

10. $\frac{4}{7}$
    $+ \frac{6}{11}$
    ———

11. $\frac{7}{8}$
    $+ \frac{5}{9}$
    ———

12. $4\frac{3}{7}$
    $+ 1\frac{4}{8}$
    ———

13. $\frac{6}{9}$
    $+ 1\frac{7}{15}$
    ———

14. $\frac{9}{14}$
    $+ \frac{7}{9}$
    ———

15. $\frac{5}{6}$
    $- \frac{1}{3}$
    ———

16. $6\frac{5}{8}$
    $- 3\frac{6}{7}$
    ———

17. $3\frac{5}{6}$
    $- 1\frac{7}{8}$
    ———

18. $5\frac{2}{7}$
    $- 2\frac{4}{5}$
    ———

19. $7\frac{3}{8}$
    $- \frac{2}{5}$
    ———

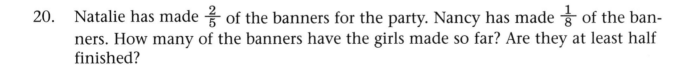

20. Natalie has made $\frac{2}{5}$ of the banners for the party. Nancy has made $\frac{1}{8}$ of the banners. How many of the banners have the girls made so far? Are they at least half finished?

Northern Africa Map. Label the countries and capitals of Northern Africa. Consult a world atlas for assistance.

Northern Africa

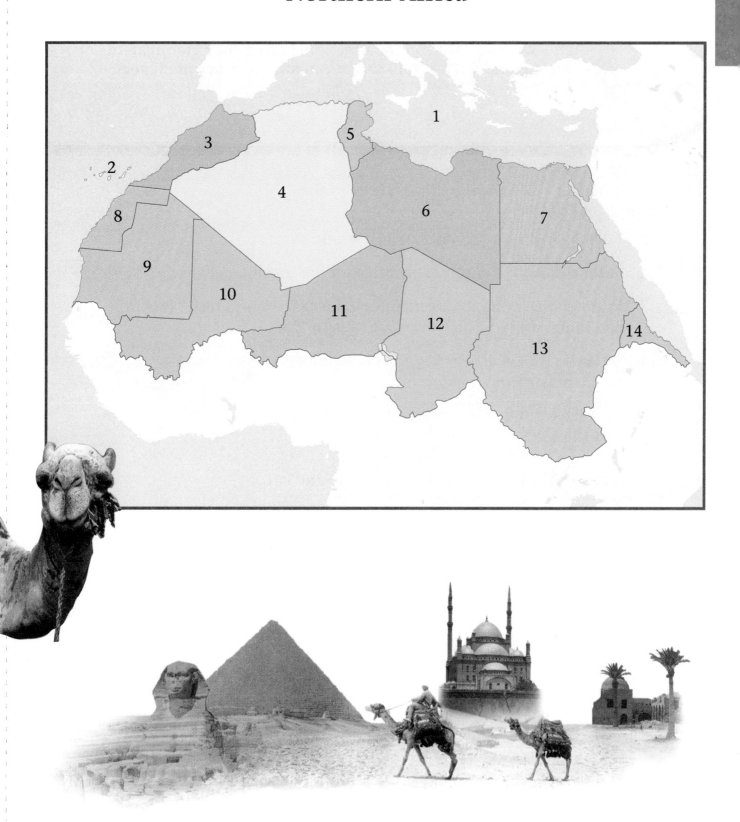

Weather. What is weather? What causes weather? How do we predict weather?

Weather is the condition of the atmosphere surrounding the earth. Several kinds of gases mix together to make up the atmosphere. Our weather is caused by heat energy, winds, moisture, and air pressure interacting in our earth's atmosphere.

Some people believe that if the groundhog sees its shadow on February 2, we will have six more weeks of winter. Another weather predictor is the saying "Red sky at night, sailor's delight. Red sky at morning, sailor take warning." Do your relatives, including your grandparents or great-grandparents, follow any folkloric weather predictors?

Decide whether each statement below is true or false.
Write T for true, F for false.

_____ 1. A barometer is used to measure temperature.

_____ 2. Carbon dioxide is largely responsible for the greenhouse effect.

_____ 3. In the summer, the continental tropical air mass forms over Mexico and brings dry, hot air to the southwestern U.S.

_____ 4. Infrared rays are absorbed by the ozone layer, which protects the earth.

_____ 5. Sleet ranges in diameter from 5 to 75 mm and falls as precipitation.

Write the letter for the best answer on the line to the left.

____ 6. When air is warmed, what happens to its density?
    A. decreases   C. triples
    B. remains the same   D. increases some

____ 7. To measure humidity is to measure
    A. air pressure.   C. ozone.
    B. water vapor.   D. temperature.

____ 8. When the altitude increases, what happens to air pressure?
    A. remains the same   C. decreases
    B. decreases, then begins to increase   D. increases

____ 9. Water boils at _____ on the Celsius scale.
    A. 121°   C. 220°
    B. 32°   D. 100°

____10. Which of the following winds has the greatest speed?
    A. hurricane   C. land breeze
    B. tornado   D. cyclone

A *clause* is a group of words that contains a subject and a verb. An *independent clause* is a clause that can act or stand alone as a complete sentence. A *dependent clause* is one that cannot act or stand alone as a complete thought. One type of dependent clause is a *subordinate clause*. A subordinate clause begins with a subordinating conjunction (such as *when*, *if*, or *because*). In the following sentences, circle the subordinate or dependent clause.

Need Help? Check Out Grammar Links at www.summerbrains.com

1. Thanksgiving has been a famous American tradition since it began in the early 1600s.
2. If it rains again today, we cannot go outside and paint the sky during art class.
3. Did you do the homework on page 398 that Mr. Barksdale told us to do?
4. Even though our team tried hard to win the championship, we still came home without medals.
5. My algebra book that I lost yesterday on the bus was found and turned in to the principal.
6. Pam knew the right answers because she stayed up late last night to study and review.
7. If my father doesn't pick me up at school, I'm riding home with Jason and Angie.
8. Our house, which is the only white house on the block, is listed for sale in the newspaper.
9. While Randy cut and raked the grass, Dan trimmed bushes and planted new flowers.

A *narrative paragraph* is one in which you "tell" how a person or a situation changes over a span of time. For example, what happened after your favorite pet died? How do you fix a flat on your bike? What caused the Civil Rights marches led by Dr. Martin Luther King, Jr.? In answering these questions, you are narrating (or telling). Narrative paragraphs are used to tell stories and explain processes or causes and effects. Write a narrative paragraph. You might consider these topics: getting a part-time job, washing a pet, watching your first movie, or embarrassing yourself.

_____
_____
_____
_____
_____
_____
_____
_____
_____
_____

Multiplying Fractions with Whole Numbers.

When multiplying a fraction by a whole number you must give the whole number a denominator of 1. This changes the whole number to a fraction without changing its value. Complete the problems by following the usual steps for multiplying fractions. Note that the word *of* is often used in multiplication problems that involve fractions instead of the x symbol. Remember, *of* means *multiply*. Always remember to reduce your answer to simplest terms if necessary.

1. $\frac{2}{3}$ x 16 = ___   2. $\frac{5}{8}$ x 20 = ___   3. $\frac{4}{5}$ x 10 = ___   4. $\frac{7}{8}$ x 32 = ___   5. $\frac{4}{9}$ x 18 = ___

6. $\frac{2}{5}$ x 40 = ___   7. $\frac{3}{4}$ x 24 = ___   8. $\frac{3}{5}$ x 15 = ___   9. $\frac{6}{7}$ x 42 = ___   10. $\frac{1}{7}$ x 21 = ___

11. $\frac{5}{12}$ x 60 = ___   12. $\frac{2}{9}$ x 64 = ___   13. $\frac{6}{15}$ x 30 = ___   14. $\frac{3}{17}$ x 59 = ___   15. $\frac{11}{18}$ x 64 = ___

Solve the word problems below.

16. Denise has 20 pets. Of the pets $\frac{2}{5}$ are rabbits, $\frac{1}{2}$ are fish, and $\frac{1}{10}$ are dogs. How many of each does she have?

17. Melanie earned $40.00. She saved $\frac{1}{4}$ of it. She plans to donate $\frac{1}{2}$ of the remaining amount to her school fund raiser. How much will she donate?

18. Tanner has 36 polished rocks. He put $\frac{1}{4}$ of them in a jar for a science experiment. He plans to give $\frac{4}{9}$ of them to a friend. How many will he have left?

Sub-Saharan Africa Map. On a separate sheet of paper, use the numbers to label the countries and capitals of Sub-Saharan Africa. Consult a world atlas for assistance.

Sub-Saharan Africa

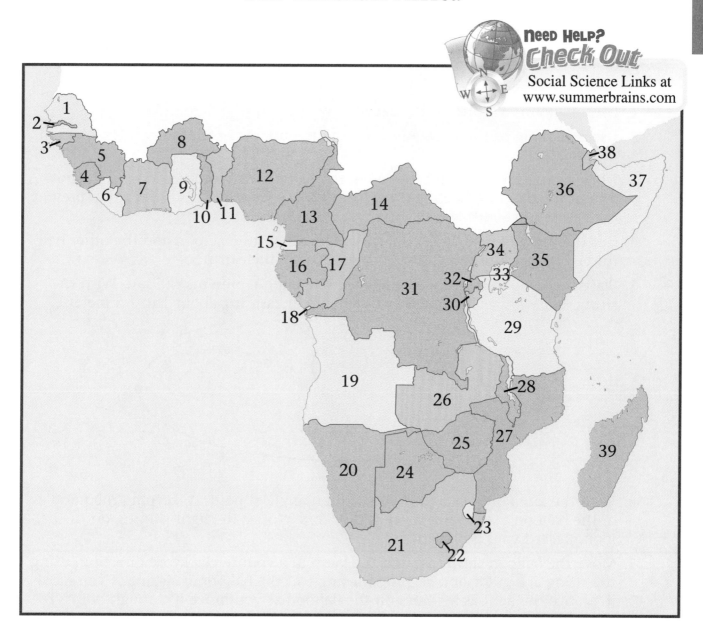

The Earth's Seasons. In most locations on the earth, the year is divided into four seasons: winter, spring, summer, and autumn. In this experiment, you will discover what causes the earth's seasons.

string (about 4 meters)   tape   scissors
drinking straw   balloon   marking pen
lamp with a bright lightbulb

1. Use a balloon to represent the earth; blow it up until it is round.

2. Use a marking pen to draw a line around the middle of the balloon to represent the equator.

3. Draw a small circle around the top of the balloon and another around the bottom of the balloon, labeling them N and S respectively. The circles will represent the North and South Poles.

4. Cut the straw in half. Tape one half to the top of the balloon and the other half to the bottom. The straw represents the axis of the earth.

5. Place the lamp in the center of a table. The lamp represents the sun. With the string, make an oval path around the lamp, measuring about 1 to 1.5 meters.

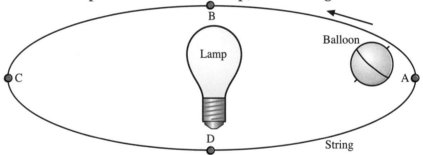

6. With the lamp on, place the balloon at an angle at point A, keeping the middle of the balloon at the same level as the lamp. Notice the light shining on the balloon. Record your observations.

7. Move the balloon slowly around the lamp in a counterclockwise direction, using the string as a guide and keeping the angle of the balloon constant as you move it. Notice the light as it shines on the balloon as you move it through points B, C, and D. Record your data.

8. Returning the balloon to point A, hold the balloon upright. The middle of the balloon should be at the same level as the lamp.

9. Again, move the balloon around the lamp through points B, C, and D, and notice the light shining on the balloon at each point. Record your observations.

Conclusion: Which point—A, B, C, or D—represents summer in the northern hemisphere? ____ Which point represents summer in the southern hemisphere? ____ At which point would the northern hemisphere have spring? ____ What season would the southern hemisphere have at the same time? ____ What causes the earth's four seasons? _____

Subject-Verb Agreement. A verb must agree in number with its subject. This means that if the subject is singular, the verb must also be singular. If the subject is plural, then the verb would be plural. In the following sentences, circle the correct verb form in parentheses. Then, on the lines provided, indicate if the verb is singular (s) or plural (p).

1. My English teacher (comes, come) from a little town in Utah. _____

2. There (was, were) three tennis rackets on the floor before break. _____

3. The ornaments on the Christmas tree (creates, create) a visual sensation. _____

4. My favorite collection of pottery (is, are) found in the Brazilian shop. _____

5. Birds that migrate south each winter (is, are) interesting animals to study. _____

6. Everyone in the band (was, were) on time for the competition. _____

7. Many of the students who live near me (walks, walk) to school every day. _____

8. Meike (don't, doesn't) bring her book to class on Tuesday and Friday. _____

9. Jeremy (shows, show) great potential as a writer. _____

10. Wes and Frank (was, were) at the soccer game last Saturday morning. _____

Possessives. The possessive case of a noun or pronoun shows ownership. Usually, to form the possessive an apostrophe is added. However, the possessive pronouns *its*, *hers*, *theirs*, and *yours* do *not* have apostrophes. Read the following sentences and make any necessary corrections to the possessive.

11. Everyones opinion counts in Mrs. Duncan's Spanish class.

12. Three boys boots were found on the field after the game. (Note: 3 boys, not 1 boy)

13. One boys boot was found in the stadium after the game. (Note: 1 boy)

14. The childrens games were too silly for someone like Grayson.

15. The girls parents were glad they had come to school to see the girls on the soccer team.

16. All of the cities mayors from across the U.S. met in Washington, D.C.

17. The little puppys leg seemed to be hurt as it ran slowly with the other puppies.

18. In an hours time my mother can bake a cake and prepare dinner for four people.

19. Mikes sweater came from Scotland, a country north of England in the United Kingdom.

20. Even though the old cars two headlights are broken, we may still buy the old junker.

Renaming and Comparing Fractions.

Fractions, equivalent fractions, or proportions are often alike because they represent equal amounts stated in different ways. Using logical thinking about the factors will help determine the equivalent answer. Rename the following fractions by finding the equivalent fraction.

1. $\frac{7}{8} = \frac{14}{}$ 2. $\frac{4}{6} = \frac{2}{}$ 3. $\frac{4}{8} = \frac{2}{}$ 4. $\frac{2}{14} = \frac{10}{}$ 5. $\frac{3}{5} = \frac{}{100}$

6. $\frac{1}{6} = \frac{}{18}$ 7. $\frac{5}{} = \frac{35}{28}$ 8. $\frac{3}{7} = \frac{}{56}$ 9. $\frac{}{24} = \frac{4}{12}$ 10. $\frac{4}{48} = \frac{1}{}$

Decide if these fractions are indeed equivalent by answering Yes or No.

11. $\frac{2}{5} = \frac{3}{9}$ 12. $\frac{5}{8} = \frac{10}{16}$ 13. $\frac{4}{9} = \frac{3}{10}$ 14. $\frac{15}{45} = \frac{5}{15}$

15. $\frac{7}{8} = \frac{9}{12}$ 16. $\frac{4}{11} = \frac{3}{16}$ 17. $\frac{14}{28} = \frac{1}{2}$ 18. $\frac{3}{26} = \frac{7}{15}$

Compare using these symbols: >, <, or =.

19. $\frac{1}{2}$ $\frac{2}{3}$ 20. $\frac{4}{9}$ $\frac{3}{5}$ 21. $\frac{6}{10}$ $\frac{1}{3}$ 22. $\frac{7}{13}$ $\frac{4}{9}$ 23. $\frac{4}{5}$ $\frac{2}{17}$

24. $\frac{3}{6}$ $\frac{12}{24}$ 25. $\frac{3}{8}$ $\frac{2}{11}$ 26. $\frac{4}{8}$ $\frac{12}{24}$ 27. $\frac{9}{72}$ $\frac{1}{8}$ 28. $\frac{3}{7}$ $\frac{6}{14}$

29. Mark scored $\frac{4}{10}$ of the total points in the game, and Jimmy scored $\frac{1}{3}$. Who scored more points in the game?

30. Ann has sold $\frac{12}{19}$ of the tickets she had to sell, while Page has sold $\frac{5}{8}$. Who has sold more of her tickets?

Grade 7–8   24   www.summerbridgeactivities.com

Middle East Map. There are several countries in the Middle East with fluid boundaries, either because of shifting politics or shifting sands. Label the numbered countries and their capitals. Refer to an atlas for assistance.

Middle East

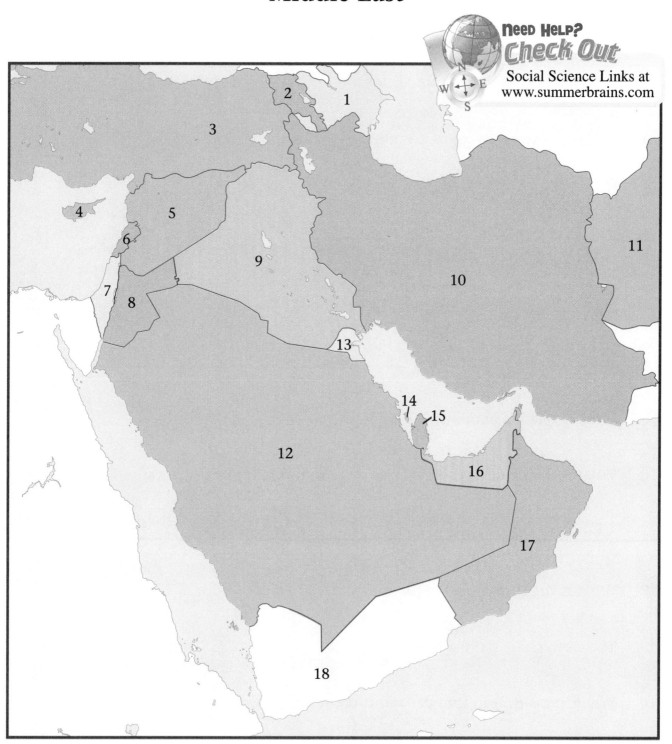

Weather or Not You Know Trivia! Are you a weather expert? See how many points you can score. You may need a reference book to help you. *Possible Score:* <u>45</u>

1. What are the names of the four layers of the earth's atmosphere? (8 Points)

2. A person who studies weather is called a what? (2 Points)

3. Who discovered that a thundercloud generates electricity? (4 Points)

4. What are the seven colors, in order, of the rainbow? (7 Points)

5. How do clouds form? (2 Points)

6. What is the most common form of precipitation? (2 Points)

7. In what country are most tornadoes found? (2 Points)

8. The southeastern part of the U.S. is found in what climate region? (2 Points)

9. What is relative humidity? (2 Points)

10. What is the name of the top layer of a tropical rain forest? (2 Points)

11. Name three factors that determine climate regions. (6 Points)

12. What is the climate region for your state? (2 Points)

13. The earth's axis is tilted at an angle of _____ degrees. (2 Points)

14. Where on earth can thunderstorms occur almost every day? (2 Points)

I scored _____ points on the weather trivia!

Writing an Essay. An essay has three main parts: introduction, body, and conclusion. A short essay often has four or five paragraphs.

The first paragraph is called the *introduction*. The purpose of the introduction is to present the main idea of the whole essay. In other words, what are you writing about?

The *body* of the essay has at least two or three paragraphs. The information in the body of the paper supports what you have stated as your main idea in the introductory paragraph. Each one of your paragraphs in the body supports the main idea in the introduction. Therefore, if you have broken down your main idea into three aspects, you would have three supporting paragraphs in the body.

The purpose of the *conclusion* is to bring your essay to a close. In this short paragraph, you want to restate the main idea that you expressed in the introductory paragraph.

Once you know what you are going to write about and before you actually begin to write, there are a few things you should do. First, brainstorm your topic and main idea. Then, make a rough outline of what you wrote on your brainstorming page. These two steps can help to organize and focus your thoughts once you begin your rough draft.

The rough draft is just what the name suggests. Don't be afraid to make mistakes. Follow your outline and write your draft without revising. Once the rough draft is written, then you can go back and begin to revise and edit.

On the following lines, write an informative essay on the Olympic Games. First, do some research on the Olympic Games, which began in 776 B.C. in Greece. In your essay, show how the Olympic Games today differ from or compare to the games in early Greece. (You may need another piece of paper.)

Adding, Subtracting, Multiplying, and Dividing with Mixed Numbers.

When working with mixed numbers it is often necessary to change the mixed number to an improper fraction. Then you can go through the usual process according to the operation you are doing. Always check your answer to be sure it is in simplest form.

need Help?
Check Out
Math Links at
www.summerbrains.com

1. $2\frac{1}{5} + 3\frac{1}{5} =$

2. $3\frac{5}{8} + 1\frac{4}{7} =$

3. $2\frac{7}{10} + 5\frac{4}{12} =$

4. $6\frac{3}{5} - 2\frac{1}{5} =$

5. $7\frac{4}{5} + 4\frac{1}{9} =$

6. $8\frac{6}{10} - 3\frac{2}{8} =$

7. $4\frac{2}{3} + 1\frac{4}{5} =$

8. $12\frac{4}{5} - 3\frac{1}{2} =$

9. $7\frac{6}{8} \times 3\frac{4}{9} =$

10. $12\frac{1}{4} \div 3\frac{5}{8} =$

11. $10\frac{2}{3} \div 4\frac{1}{7} =$

12. $5\frac{7}{8} \div 1\frac{1}{3} =$

Solve the following problems.

13. If a restaurant has $2\frac{1}{4}$ cherry pies, $4\frac{3}{4}$ apple pies, and $\frac{1}{2}$ of a blueberry pie remaining after dinner one night, how many pies are left?

14. If Lisa has $\frac{2}{3}$ of her homework pages done, and Jennifer has only $\frac{1}{8}$ of that amount done, how much has Jennifer completed?

15. Denise has $16\frac{2}{3}$ shares of stock in a phone company. She wants to divide them equally among 4 of her nieces. If she does this, how many shares will each niece receive?

Northern Asia Map. Label the countries and capitals for each of the numbers below. Consult a world atlas for assistance.

Northern Asia

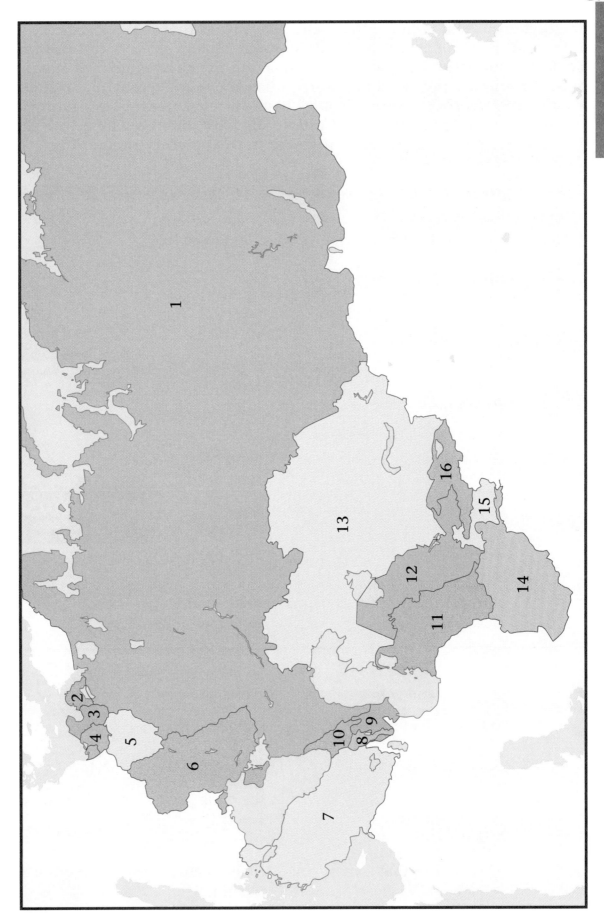

Ecology. Ecology is the branch of biology that deals with relationships between living organisms and their environment. This means that ecology is directly related to important issues of energy and conservation. Ecology deals with fossil fuels, such as coal, oil, and natural gas, and their impact on the environment. It can include the study of solar energy, wind and water, nuclear energy, geothermal energy, tidal energy, and hydrogen power. Ecology helps us recognize that everything on earth has a role or function, and instead of interfering with nature's scheme, we should find better ways of working together *with* the earth and everything in it.

Write the letter of the best answer on the line to the left.

_____ 1. Which one of the following is not a fossil fuel?
    A. sandstone   C. oil
    B. coal   D. natural gas

_____ 2. What is the source of hydroelectric power?
    A. sun   C. water
    B. turbine   D. tides

_____ 3. Which energy do green plants use?
    A. water energy   C. wind energy
    B. hydrogen energy   D. solar energy

_____ 4. What is the most common natural gas?
    A. propane   C. hydrogen
    B. methane   D. ethanol

_____ 5. Tidal power is an example of
    A. wind energy.   C. solar energy.
    B. water energy.   D. nonrenewable energy.

_____ 6. Fossil fuels came from which of the following?
    A. rocks   C. heat and pressure
    B. plants and animals D. wood and clay

_____ 7. Which one of the following is a renewable resource?
    A. wood   C. coal
    B. oil   D. natural gas

_____ 8. Animals and plants that lived in the oceans formed which fossil fuel?
    A. bituminous coal   C. wood
    B. anthracite   D. oil

_____ 9. The element that is most abundant as an energy source on our planet is
    A. carbon.   C. oxygen.
    B. hydrogen.   D. nitrogen.

Modifiers. A *modifier* describes or limits the meaning of another word. Modifiers are adjectives and adverbs that may be used to compare things. Read the following sentences. Draw an X through the modifier that needs to be removed from the sentence. If a new modifier is needed, write it on the line.

1. We don't hardly have time to write a sentence. _____

2. Of the two singers, Mariah Carey has the best voice. _____

3. Your answer doesn't make no difference to her. _____

4. My sisters work even more harder than I do. _____

5. Randy does good in all his subjects at school. _____

6. Benny is tallest. _____

7. There are so many choices, I don't know which I like more. _____

8. I couldn't hardly believe Monica said that. _____

9. Donald Duck is one of the most funniest cartoon characters. _____

10. This cake is gooder than the pie you brought. _____

11. She wore the beautifulest dress of any girl. _____

12. The zebra is more smaller than the huge elephant. _____

Conjunctions, Interjections, and Prepositions. A *conjunction* is a word used to join words or groups of words. An *interjection* is a word used to express emotion. A *preposition* is a word used to show the relationship of a noun or pronoun to another word or phrase in a sentence. Read the following sentences. If there are conjunctions, interjections, and prepositions, label them as conj, int, or prep on the lines provided.

13. The desk on the third row is my friend's seat. _____

14. Wait! It's my turn on the motorcycle. _____

15. Chris and his mother were the only ones by the stop sign. _____

16. In the front office sat the lonely little boy. _____

17. I went to the play, but I sat in the back. _____

18. Volleyball is a fun sport for boys and girls. _____

19. We left the school, and we went to the grocery store. _____

20. Wow! I passed the test. _____

Working with Decimals.

When adding or subtracting decimal numbers, it is important to align the decimal points. Often this may cause the problem to appear staggered, but in fact, it is correct. Align the following problems properly and solve.

1. 4.328
    + 1.097

2. 3.7502
    + .0814

3. .7894
    − .0325

4. 897.0352
    − 46.0231

5. 3.26
    + .278

6. 237.895
    + 30.25

7. 7.4036
    − .1437

8. 24.059
    + 1.497

9. .3862
    + 5.097

10. 4.675
    − 2.431

11. 6.987
    1.73
    + 30.25

12. 7.4036
    13.765
    + .1437

13. 24.059
    2.876
    + 1.497

14. .3862
    1.45
    + 5.097

15. 4.675
    9.56
    + 2.431

Add or subtract the following problems after setting them up correctly.

16. 45.8 + 372.01 =

17. 13.287 − 2.098 =

18. 679.73 − 4.238 =

19. .765 + 4.389 =

20. Jane ran .843 mile on her usual route on Monday. On Tuesday she ran .793 mile, and on Wednesday 1.48 miles. What was her total mileage in those three days?

21. Kelly bought 3.58 yards of fabric. She plans to make a table cover. If she uses 1.03 yards of the fabric to make napkins, how much will she have left to make the table cover?

22. Mark has 12.48 gallons of weed killer. He plans to use 2.78 gallons for Mrs. Moore's yard. He'll need 1.32 gallons for Mr. Greer's yard. After he treats these yards, how much weed killer will he have left over?

Incentive Contract Calendar

Month _____

My parents and I decided that if I complete 20 days of
Summer Bridge Activities™ 7–8 and read _____ minutes a day,
my incentive/reward will be:

_____

Child's Signature_____

Parent's Signature_____

Day 1	☐	☐	____	Day 11	☐ ☐	____
Day 2	☐	☐	____	Day 12	☐ ☐	____
Day 3	☐	☐	____	Day 13	☐ ☐	____
Day 4	☐	☐	____	Day 14	☐ ☐	____
Day 5	☐	☐	____	Day 15	☐ ☐	____
Day 6	☐	☐	____	Day 16	☐ ☐	____
Day 7	☐	☐	____	Day 17	☐ ☐	____
Day 8	☐	☐	____	Day 18	☐ ☐	____
Day 9	☐	☐	____	Day 19	☐ ☐	____
Day 10	☐	☐	____	Day 20	☐ ☐	____

Child: Put a ✔ in the ☐ for the daily activities ▭ completed.

Put a ✔ in the ☐ for the daily reading ▬ completed.

Parent: Initial the ____ for daily activities and reading your child completes.

Best Day/Vacation So Far

Write about It

Picture

Picture

Picture

Write about It

Asia/Southeast Asia Map. Label the countries and their capitals. Do not overlook the island nations that surround the mainland. Consult a world atlas for assistance.

Asia/Southeast Asia

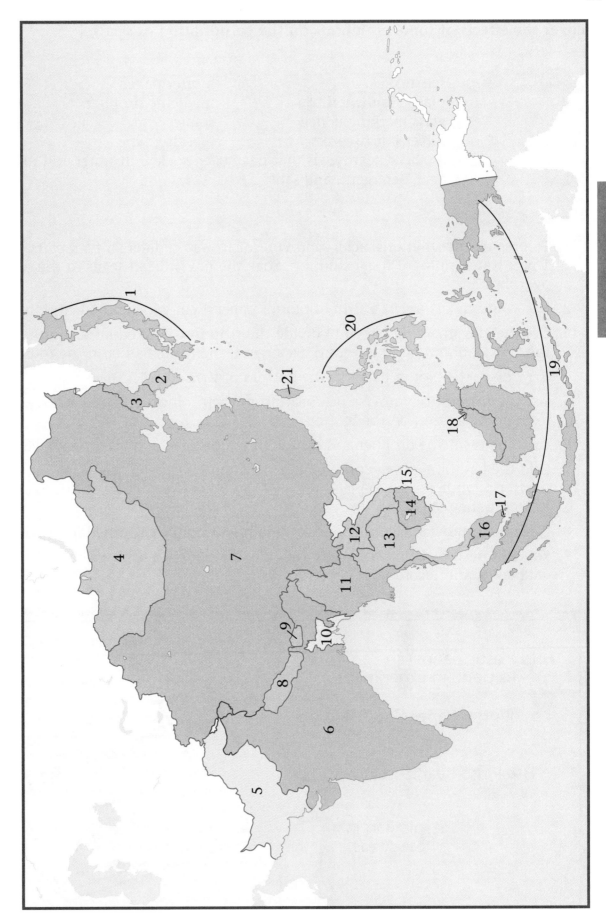

© Summer Bridge Activities™   35   Grade 7–8

Examining the Effects of Pollution on Germination. In this experiment, you will discover the effects of some pollutants on the germination of seeds.

 **Materials:**

scissors	blotter paper
plastic sandwich bag	medicine dropper
glass-marking pencil	stapler
forceps or tweezers	masking tape

4 pea or bean seeds that have been soaked in water and in solutions of acid, detergent, and salt

Procedure:

1. To prepare the solutions: acid—add vinegar to water; detergent—3 parts detergent to 1 part water; salt—10% salt solution. Soak the pea or bean seeds in the solutions overnight.

2. Use your scissors to cut a strip of blotter paper 4 cm wide and 16 cm long.

3. Use the glass-marking pencil to divide the strip into four equal sections. Then, label the first section Acid; the second, Detergent; the third, Salt; and the fourth, Control.

4. Now place the blotter paper in the bottom of the sandwich bag.

5. Use the forceps to remove a pea/bean from each solution. Place each seed in the corresponding section on the blotter.

6. Take the medicine dropper and thoroughly moisten the blotter paper with water.

7. Fold the bag carefully over the blotter paper and pea/bean seeds. Do not disturb the seeds. Use your stapler to place a row of staples between each pea/bean seed in order to secure the seed within its section.

8. Place the sandwich bag in an area where it will not be disturbed for 5 days.

9. You will need to watch the seeds each day for evidence of germination. Prepare a data table, and record your observations each day.

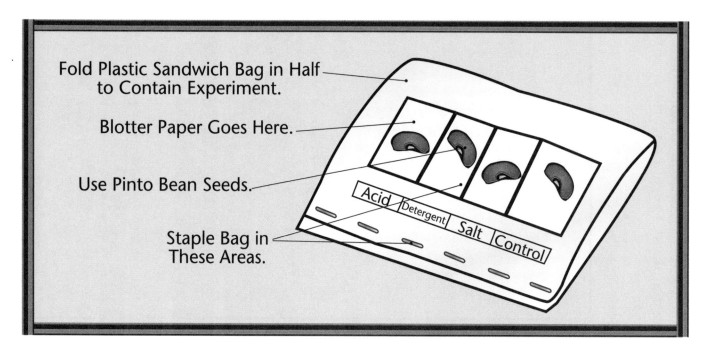

Fold Plastic Sandwich Bag in Half to Contain Experiment.

Blotter Paper Goes Here.

Use Pinto Bean Seeds.

Staple Bag in These Areas.

Acid Detergent Salt Control

Standard English is the most widely recognized form of English. It is used in formal situations, such as speeches and compositions for school, and in informal situations, such as conversation and everyday writing. Read the following groups of sentences and choose the letter of the sentence that contains an error.

____ 1. A. They bought themselves new shirts.
      B. Use less sugar.
      C. The bubble busted.

____ 2. A. He looks somewhat hungry.
      B. Do as the teacher does.
      C. Will you learn me how to water ski?

____ 3. A. This here bicycle is broken again.
      B. I just bought those two new books.
      C. Try to enjoy the movie.

____ 4. A. It's stormy.
      B. I know how come she left today.
      C. My father used to play the piano.

____ 5. A. She behaved bad.
      B. They left less juice for Ted.
      C. Jan herself bought that tie.

____ 6. A. The chair broke.
      B. Misty could of come.
      C. She sat down.

____ 7. A. They have a long way to go.
      B. That magazine has fewer pages.
      C. Your my friend.

____ 8. A. He looks as though he is tired.
      B. Their are not enough cushions.
      C. He sang well.

Diagramming Sentences. A sentence diagram is a picture of how the parts of a sentence fit together. Read the following sentences, and then diagram them in the space provided.

Example: The little boy wrote the poem.

(noun) boy | (verb) wrote | (object) poem — The / little / the

9. Erin enjoyed the plane ride.

10. Copenhagen is a great city.

11. Heather and Kevin read the book.

12. Did you go on the trip to Oslo?

13. The little baby cried loudly on the boat.

14. She looks a little tired.

15. Danielle and Jon sang and danced in the musical.

Fraction and Decimal Equivalents.

Rename each of the fractions as the decimal equivalent. In the case of a terminating decimal, use the number to the last place value. Where the decimal is repeating, you may round it to the nearest hundredth.

1. $\frac{1}{3}$ = ——

2. $\frac{1}{6}$ = ——

3. $\frac{7}{8}$ = ——

4. $\frac{3}{5}$ = ——

5. $\frac{5}{8}$ = ——

6. $\frac{2}{3}$ = ——

7. $\frac{7}{9}$ = ——

8. $\frac{6}{12}$ = ——

Rename each decimal as its fractional equivalent.

9. .8 = ——

10. .78 = ——

11. .9 = ——

12. .57 = ——

13. .06 = ——

14. .12 = ——

15. .26 = ——

16. .43 = ——

Fill in the blank with the correct number.

17. $\frac{1}{5}$ is equal to _____ tenths.

18. .72 is equal to this fraction: _____.

19. $\frac{4}{5}$ is equal to _____ tenths.

20. $\frac{2}{5}$ is equal to _____ tenths.

21. 1.25 is equal to this mixed number : _____.

22. .03 is equal to this fraction: _____.

23. $\frac{2}{9}$ is equal to _____ hundredths.

24. $\frac{3}{7}$ is equal to _____ thousandths.

25. .088 is equal to this fraction: _____.

Oceania Map. Label the countries, capitals, major islands, and island groups. Label the territories of Australia and their capitals. Label the two main islands of New Zealand. Consult a world atlas for assistance.

Oceania

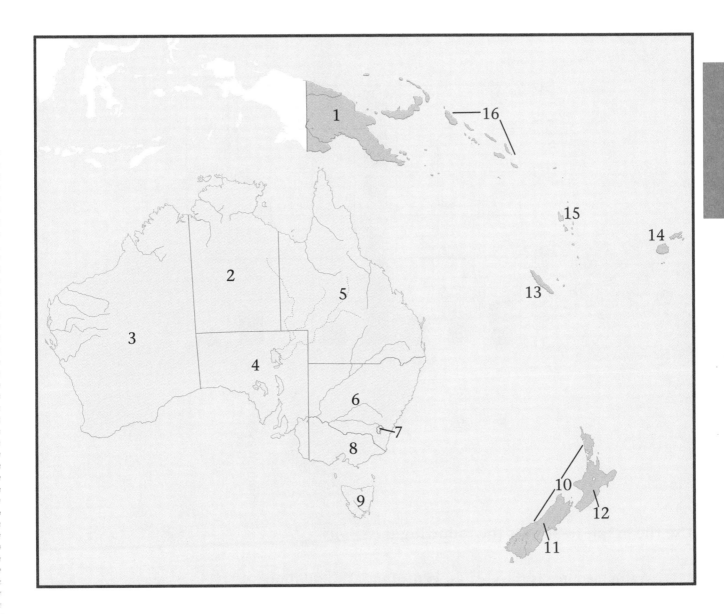

Pollution. Everyone seems to agree that *pollution* is a bad word. Pollution is the release or introduction into the environment of materials or substances that change the environment. How do you and your family contribute to pollution on Earth? How is your family finding ways to curb pollution?

The following graph reflects sources and amounts of carbon monoxide pollution emitted into the air in the United States.

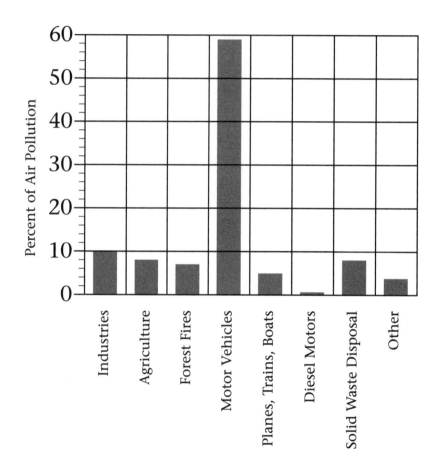

Use the graph to answer the following questions.

1. Which source is the greatest contributor to pollution? _____

2. Which source is the smallest contributor of pollution? _____

3. What percent does agriculture add to the overall pollution in the U.S.? _____

4. Which source emits about 9.7% of the carbon monoxide into the air? _____

5. Can you think of ways to decrease the percentage of motor vehicle emissions?

_____

Commas. Read the sentences below. Insert any commas where needed.

1. For lunch we are having fish French fries and lemonade.

2. The boat is heading toward Copenhagen Denmark.

3. If we miss the train in Seattle let's rent a car.

4. There were twenty-three people invited to the party but Erin said only twenty people actually came.

5. Do they still live at 101 Oak Street Decatur Alabama?

6. Heather do you want to go with us on the excursion?

7. Down the lonely dusty road we could see the sun slowly setting on the horizon.

8. The oldest member of the class is Donna who was born on July 2 1988.

9. Dr. Timothy Sanders M.D. has an office in Atlanta Georgia.

Diagramming. As you diagram the following sentences, pay special attention to the placement of prepositional phrases. These phrases can describe nouns, adjectives, or adverbs.

Example: This book by John Hayes describes the struggle for freedom.

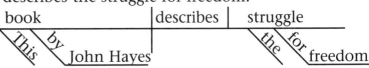

10. Mark Twain told his audiences stories about his life on the Mississippi River.

11. Tell us the story of your rescue.

12. San Marino, in the mountains of Italy, is sixteen centuries old.

13. Was Davy Crockett one of the defenders of the Alamo?

Percentages.

The best tip for remembering percentages is to think "percent means hundredths." This makes it easier to convert to decimals and fractions and vice versa.

Example: 75% is also $\frac{75}{100}$ (or simplified to $\frac{3}{4}$), and the decimal is 0.75.

1. $\frac{3}{100}$ = ___%   2. $\frac{12}{100}$ = ___%   3. $\frac{25}{100}$ = ___%   4. $\frac{84}{100}$ = ___%

Fill in the table with the correct decimal, fraction, or percent.

Percent	Fraction	Decimal
5. 17%	$\frac{17}{100}$	
6.	$\frac{39}{100}$	.39
7. 77%		.77
8. 35%	$\frac{35}{100}$	
9.	$\frac{47}{100}$	.47
10. 36%		.36
11.	$2\frac{4}{100}$	2.04
12. 138%		1.38
13. 765%	$7\frac{65}{100}$	
14.	$\frac{12}{100}$	.12

Europe Map. Label the countries and capitals of Europe. Be sure to include Andorra, San Marino, Liechtenstein, Vatican City, Malta, England, Scotland, Northern Ireland, Wales, the new republics of the former Soviet Union, and those of the former Yugoslavia. Then label the major bodies of water. Consult an atlas for assistance.

Europe

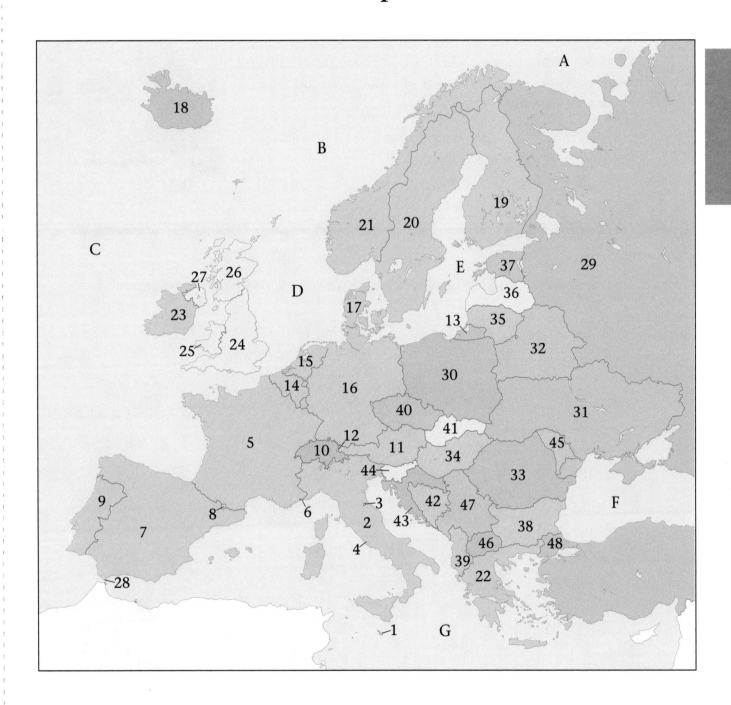

Pollution. Do you know? If the following statements are true, write T; if false, mark F.

_____ 1. Acid rain may cause water pollution, land pollution, and air pollution.

_____ 2. Did you know that air pollution can be reduced by burning wood?

_____ 3. Radioactive nuclear wastes are stored in airtight containers made of glass.

_____ 4. If the containers in which nuclear wastes are buried underground leak, the leaking wastes would first pollute the air.

_____ 5. A Ukrainian nuclear power plant in Chernobyl exploded and caught fire in 1986.

Multiple Choice: Write the letter of the best answer on the line to the left.

_____ 6. What is the most significant source of air pollution?
A. lawn mowers   C. airplanes and boats
B. acid rain   D. automobile emissions

_____ 7. If the temperature increases in the water of lakes and streams, then _____ pollution may occur.
A. solar   C. land
B. thermal   D. air

_____ 8. What is produced when rainwater mixes with pollutants?
A. air pollution   C. acid rain
B. water pollution   D. thermal pollution

_____ 9. The Exxon _Valdez_ was a (an)
A. oil tanker.   C. national park.
B. army submarine.   D. corporate airplane.

_____ 10. Which one of the following is not a fossil fuel?
A. coal   C. oil
B. nitrogen oxide   D. natural gas

Reading Comprehension. Read the following story by Rafael Martins, and then answer the questions that follow.

THE SURPRISE

It began as an ordinary day for Mark, an eleven-year-old boy, who had just gotten out of school for the day. His best friend, Daniel, was walking with him. "Hey Mark," said Daniel, "wanna go to my house for a while and play hoops?"

"Nah, my dad was going to show me a surprise today after school, so I'm going straight home to find out what it is," exclaimed Mark.

"Oh," mumbled Daniel, "will you call me when you find out what it is?"

"Sure."

"I'll be waiting by the phone," yelled Daniel, walking away. "See ya."

"Bye!" yelled Mark. "Hmm, I wonder what Dad's surprise is?" he thought to himself, pondering all kinds of things.

As he was walking along, a black car pulled up from the adjacent street and began following Mark. Noticing, Mark thought, "I wonder why he's following me?"

Becoming a little unsure, Mark started walking off course and headed back to his school. But the car followed. Mark turned left and right on every street, but the car continued behind him. Beginning to worry, Mark picked up his pace and began to jog. The car sped up.

Trying to look back to determine who was driving the car, Mark could only see tinted windows and a shadowy figure. This is when he started to panic. In a split second he ran through a stranger's backyard and jumped over the fence. Then he hid behind a bush and quietly watched the car speed by the house.

He stayed near the bush for a few minutes just to make sure the suspicious car did not come back. And it didn't.

Finally, with caution, Mark sprinted across the street and ran all the way to his neighborhood. On every corner he would watch for any sign of the car. Furthermore, he avoided the main street by walking through his neighbors' backyards.

When he was within three blocks of his house, he began to run as fast as he could. When he arrived at his house, he couldn't believe his eyes. The black car was stationed in his driveway. Mark stopped, holding his breath. The car door opened. Again, he couldn't believe his eyes. It was his dad getting out of the car. "Surprise," his dad shouted to Mark.

"Dad?" Mark said in amazement and shock.

"I went to pick you up after school in the new car, but you ran off. I couldn't find you, and then I couldn't catch you," his dad said laughing.

"Phew!" Mark sighed.

"Hop in! I'll take you on a little ride around town," his dad said, smiling.

"Thanks, Dad," Mark said, getting in and feeling secure once again.

1. Where did Daniel want to go to play hoops? _____

2. How did Mark finally get home?_____

3. What was the surprise? _____

4. What color is the car? _____

5. Why did Mark act strangely on his way home from school? _____

6. Do you think the dad was right in following Mark in the car? Why or why not? ____

_____

Using Percentages.

Percentages help us find portions of amounts, such as taxes, discounts, or interest. They are computed as decimal numbers, and often they are found in phrases using "of," which means multiply.

Figure the amounts with the information given.

1. 36% of 400 = _____   2. 40% of 56 = _____

3. 20% of 75 = _____   4. 78% of 975 = _____

5. 12% of 84 = _____   6. 29% of 530 = _____

7. 45% of 99 = _____   8. 72% of 100 = _____

Figure the discount price.

9. Mary went to a store to buy a coat. The price was $180.00. The sale sign indicated that it was on sale for 30% off the original price. What is the price of the coat before tax?

10. Wade bought a weight bench on sale for $175.00. It was originally $300.00. What was the percent discount?

11. Mark bought a car for $34,900.00. The tax on the car was 5%. After tax, what was the total price of the car?

12. Bob received a letter from a company indicating he would be getting a 5% dividend on his stock. He has $4,800.00 worth of stock with the company. How much will his dividend payment be?

Using Latitude and Longitude. *Latitude* measures the number of degrees and direction (north or south) of the equator a place is located. *Longitude* measures the number of degrees and direction (east or west) of the prime meridian a place is located. Use a colored pencil to trace and label the equator and the prime meridian. Use a different colored pencil to trace and label the Arctic and Antarctic Circles, the tropics of Cancer and Capricorn, and the International Date Line (assume that it follows one line of longitude).

For each latitude and longitude below, (1) locate and label the city on the map, and (2) place the name of the city in the blank below. Use your atlas to help accomplish this task.

City	Latitude	Longitude
1. _____	30°N	31°E
2. _____	41°S	175°E
3. _____	34°S	18°E
4. _____	52°N	13°E
5. _____	33°N	117°W
6. _____	42°N	87°W
7. _____	22°N	114°E
8. _____	49°N	2°E
9. _____	40°N	116°E
10. _____	35°S	58°W
11. _____	44°N	79°W
12. _____	10°N	67°W

For each city listed below, (1) plot and label the city on the map, and (2) record the latitude and longitude on the chart below. Again use your atlas.

City	Latitude	Longitude
13. Rio de Janeiro	_____	_____
14. London	_____	_____
15. Bombay	_____	_____
16. Johannesburg	_____	_____
17. Tokyo	_____	_____
18. Mexico City	_____	_____
19. Rome	_____	_____
20. Moscow	_____	_____
21. Los Angeles	_____	_____
22. New York City	_____	_____
23. Canberra	_____	_____
24. Ottawa	_____	_____

Conserving Resources on Earth.

Choose the word in the word group that does not belong. As you think of which word to eliminate, think in terms of conservation and the earth's resources.

1.   A. coal   C. natural gas
      B. oil   D. solar energy
      Reason: _____

2.   A. bicycle   C. bus
      B. subway   D. train
      Reason: _____

3.   A. reused resources   C. renewable resources
      B. recycled resources   D. nonrenewable resources
      Reason: _____

4.   A. water   C. buildings
      B. oil   D. air
      Reason: _____

5.   A. air   C. thermal
      B. water   D. land
      Reason: _____

Match the following words on the left with the statements on the right.

_____ 6. oil

_____ 7. aluminum

_____ 8. carbon monoxide

_____ 9. acid rain

_____ 10. recycling

A. a poisonous emission

B. one way the solid waste problem can be reduced

C. fuel that cannot be easily replaced by nature

D. one substance that can be recycled

E. formed when water vapor in the air mixes with sulfur oxides

Underlining, Quotation Marks, Hyphen, and Dash. Read the following sentences, correctly punctuating each one. Make sure the quotation marks are in the correct place relative to other marks of punctuation.

1. The first chapter in Walden is entitled Economy.

2. As a baby-sitter I have read the children's book The Little Mermaid at least ten times.

3. Leave your binoculars at home, suggested Mrs. Haynes. Your ears will be more helpful than your eyes on this field trip.

4. Our family is planning to take a week's vacation in mid July to visit Yellowstone Park.

5. Curtis Mr. Williams, I mean will be our new principal at the high school next year.

6. At eight o'clock this morning, said the reporter, someone broke into the bank and escaped with 10,000 dollars.

7. The word Tennessee has four e's, two n's, and two s's.

8. The name of our overnight ferry from Copenhagen to Oslo was the Scandinavian Queen.

Colons and Semicolons. Read the following sentences, and on the lines provided write the word(s) in each sentence where a colon or semicolon is required.

_____ 9. In 1906 one of the worst earthquakes in history occurred in the Pacific Ocean off South America its Richter scale measurement was 8.9.

_____ 10. If you are going to bake the cake, you'll need several other items chocolate, eggs, sugar, sour cream, and flour.

_____ 11. From 7 00 A.M. until 8 00 P.M., Eric sells school supplies in the room next to the front office.

_____ 12. I have received postcards from Budapest, Hungary Sydney, Australia, and London, England.

_____ 13. Laura felt shy in the new class however, she soon made some new friends.

_____ 14. Samantha likes to act her older brother gets stage fight.

_____ 15. The minister, priest, and rabbi discussed Genesis 1 26 and 3 14.

Interest.

Need Help?
Check Out
Math Links at
www.summerbrains.com

Interest is money paid for the use of money from a bank or other lender. The *principal* is the amount of money borrowed. The *rate* is the percentage established by the lender to calculate the amount of interest the borrower will owe. The *time* is the duration of the loan. For the purpose of this activity, all of the interest is based on a yearly basis. The formula to find accrued interest is P x R x T = I (Principal x Rate x Time = Interest).

Use the formula above to find the amount of interest for each scenario below and to fill in the chart.

1. Mr. Gaddy bought a new car for $65,000.00. He financed the car at a rate of 12% for 4 years. How much will the interest be on this loan?

2. Mrs. Lee purchased a new house for $187,000.00 and financed it for 30 years. Her bank gave her an interest rate of 8%. What will be the amount of interest she will pay the bank on this loan?

3. Mr. Keung has a credit card with a bank that charges 18% interest. He has carried $500.00 on the card for 1 year. How much interest has he paid on the $500.00 in this 1 year?

Using the formula, make the necessary computations for the missing items in the chart.

PRINCIPAL	RATE	TIME	INTEREST
$200.00	5%	3 years	$30.00
1. $830.00	4%	2 years	
2. $64.00	8%	1 year	
3. $1,200.00	6%	5 years	
4. $300.00	9%	4 years	
5. $424.00	7%	2 years	
6. $78.00	4%	1 year	
7. $650.00	9%	1 year	
8. $2,000.00	5%	6 years	
9. $1,800.00	11%	4 years	
10. $25,000.00	16%	15 years	
11. $450,000.00	18%	30 years	
12. $7,500.00	21%	5 years	
13. $32,000.00	15%	12 years	
14. $1,000,000.00	28%	35 years	

Dot Map. One type of thematic map is a dot map. This map on population distribution in Southeast Asia uses dots to show clusters of population in the region. Each dot represents 100,000 people. Use the map below to answer these questions.

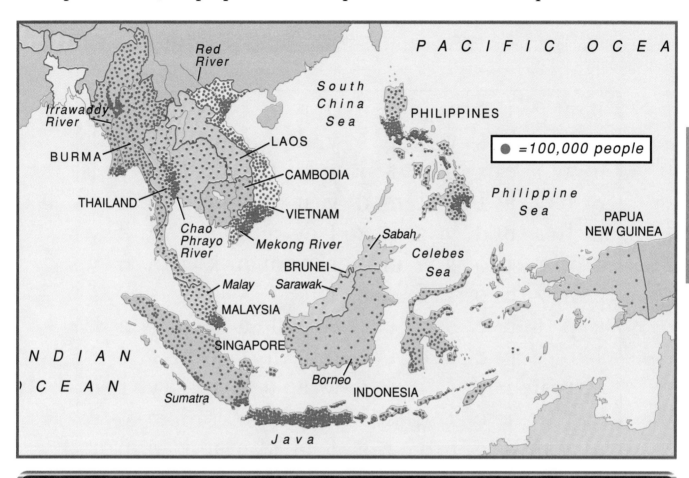

1. In continental Southeast Asia, around what geographic feature do populations cluster? _____

2. Name four major rivers of Southeast Asia. _____

3. According to the map, do more people live in Malaysia or Indonesia? _____

4. Which islands appear to be the most sparsely populated?_____

5. What specific area appears to have the greatest population density?_____

6. According to the map, which country has the greater population density, the Philippines or Indonesia? _____

7. Which countries in continental Southeast Asia appear to have the most even population distribution? _____

8. What do the dots on the map signify? _____

Matter. Matter is anything and everything around you. It is what you see and often what you cannot see. Matter is the universe, plants, animals, soil, iron, oxygen, carbon monoxide, and air. However, all matter does have the general properties of mass, weight, volume, and density.

Locate and circle 20 terms related to matter. The words may be written across, up, down, or diagonally.

```
t h g i e w p a n d p r c f a x z l
c e s b s v j l s y d e o n w r e l
h x j e x o r t j w u t n z f e v l
e r v a t j l m d y u t d s n d a p
m f a b d y s u z l w a e j o e p y
i v r j q s v m t r v m n k i n o v
c a z e p l b e u i c t s h t s r f
a p t b e s o l i d o f a y a i a h
l o e p c z d t c n q n t f m t t i
c r u l t f i i y w a t i g i y i n
h i e i c i q n i a w j o r l p o e
a z m q c p i g g f m s n a b s n r
n a u u z l z p r p a d n v u x g t
g t l i k a i o i k o m a i s o a i
e i o d u s o i q z n i r t x o s a
w o v p t m t n h q o n n y e w c n
h n u c d a l t o m q b h t m a s s
d s l s t n i o p g n i l i o b v o
```

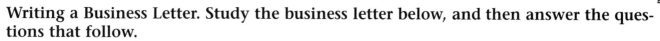

Writing a Business Letter. Study the business letter below, and then answer the questions that follow.

(1)   Angela Taylor
(2)   108 West Pine Street
(3)   Portland ME 04104
(4)   June 1, 1998

(5)   Forest Service
(6)   U.S. Department of Agriculture
(7)   Washington D.C. 20250

(8)   Dear Sir or Madam,

(9)   My seventh grade class is doing research on national forests in
(10)   America. I have been assigned to find out what forests are located in
(11)   North Carolina. My teacher suggested I write to your department.

(12)   If you can send me any information on national forests in North
(13)   Carolina, I would appreciate it very much. Thank you.

(14)   sincerely.

(15)   Angela T.

Questions.

_____ 1. In lines 1, 2, 3, and 4, there are errors in two lines. In what lines are the errors?
    A. lines 1 and 4   C. lines 2 and 3
    B. lines 1 and 3   D. lines 2 and 4

_____ 2. Which corrects the error in line 5, 6, or 7?
    A. U.S., Department of Agriculture   C. Washington, D.C.
    B. Forest Service: D. no error

_____ 3. There are two errors in lines 8, 12, and 13. Choose the corrections below.
    A. Madam: and no indent line 12   C. Sir; and indent line 12
    B. Dear, Sir: and indent line 12   D. no error in line 8 and indent line 12

_____ 4. Choose the corrections for lines 14 and 15
    A. Sincerely. and Angela Taylor   C. sincerely, and Angela Taylor
    B. Sincerely, and Angela T.   D. Sincerely, and Angela Taylor

Geometry.

Identify the following figures.

1.

_____

2.

_____

3.

_____

4.

_____

Identify the type of angle shown.

5.

_____

6.

_____

7.

_____

8.

_____

In the space below draw examples of the three types of triangles.

9. right

10. scalene

11. isosceles

Buying Big Burgers. Use the following Junior Achievement-generated chart to compare currency exchange rates between U.S. dollars and several other countries' currencies. Then use the exchange rates to calculate some specific conversions.

CURRENCY TRADING
Exchange Rates

Country	What Foreign Currency Equals in U.S. Dollars	What $1 U.S. Equals in Foreign Currency
Australia	$ .57	1.77 dollars (Australian)
Chile	$.0014	711 pesos
China	$ .12	8.35 yuan
France	$ 1.01	.99 euros
Israel	$ .21	4.69 shekels

1. Explain how the value of the Australian and U.S. dollars compare. _____

_____

_____

2. Complete the Super Burger chart below. The first one has been completed as an example.

 **The Super Burger Chart**

Your $5	x	What $1 U.S. = Equals in Foreign Currency	What $5 U.S. − Equals in Foreign Currency	Cost of Super Burger in Foreign Currency	=	Your Change in Foreign Currency	x	What Foreign Currency Equals in U.S. Dollars	=	Your Change in U.S. Dollars	Cost of Super Burger in U.S. Dollars
A. U.S. $5	x	1.77 dollars = (Australian)	8.85 dollars − (Australian)	2.72 dollars = (Australian)		6.13 dollars (Australian)	x	$ .57	=	$3.49	$1.51
B. U.S. $5	x	711 pesos =	____ pesos −	1700 pesos =		____ pesos	x	$ .0014	=	$2.60	____
C. U.S. $5	x	8.35 yuan =	41.75 yuan −	9.6 yuan =		____ yuan	x	$ .12	=	$3.86	____
D. U.S. $5	x	.99 euros =	4.95 euros −	3 euros =		1.95 euros	x	$ 1.01	=	$_.___	____
E. U.S. $5	x	4.69 shekels =	____ shekels −	12.5 shekels =		10.95 shekels	x	$ .21	=	$2.30	____

What Matters? Stretch your brain matter to see if you know the answers to the following questions or statements.

Need Help? **Check Out** Science Links at www.summerbrains.com

1. Define *mixture*, *solution*, and *element*.

2. What is the difference between a heterogeneous and a homogeneous mixture?

3. Since oil does not dissolve in water, it is said to be _____.

4. Can you name or list at least 20 chemical symbols?

   _____

   _____

5. What is a compound?

6. What is the difference between an atom and a molecule?

7. What is the chemical equation for water?

8. What was John Dalton's atomic theory?

9. What are 3 main subatomic particles found in atoms?

10. Which 2 subatomic particles are found inside the nucleus of an atom?

11. What determines the atomic number of an element?

12. What determines the mass number of an element?

13. Where are electrons found in the atom?

14. Gold has an atomic number of 79. What does the 79 mean?

Research Paper. Study the following three parts of a research paper: outline, parenthetical documentation, and works cited. Answer the questions that follow each part.

I. OUTLINE

REDISCOVERING THE TITANIC

I. Maiden Voyage

II. Disaster on the Ocean
   A. Iceberg
   B. Flooding
   C. Lifeboats

III. Discovery in the Ocean
   A. Jason, Jr., was the underwater robot.
   B. New Information

IV. Hollywood Movie

1. What do we call the topics *Maiden Voyage, Disaster on the Ocean, Discovery in the Ocean*, and *Hollywood Movie*? _____

2. Should the V in *Voyage* in Part I and the O in *Ocean* in Part II be capitalized? _____

3. The two topics under Part III are incorrectly written. How would you write them correctly? _____

II. PARENTHETICAL DOCUMENTATION

In just a matter of minutes, I went from remembering a night of great celebration and happiness to one of great fear and terror (White 85).

4. What does the 85 represent in the example above?_____

5. What does the word *White* represent in the same example?_____

III. WORKS CITED

Murphy, Jamie. "Down into the Deep." Time
11 Aug. 1986: 48–54.

6. Who is *Murphy, Jamie* in the Works Cited example above? _____

7. What does *48-54* stand for in the example above? _____

8. What is the name of the article from which information was taken for the example above?_____

Perimeter and Surface Area.

Find the perimeter and area of each figure.

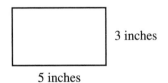

3 inches

5 inches

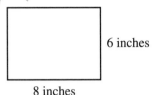

6 inches

8 inches

1. perimeter _____

2. area _____

3. perimeter _____

4. area _____

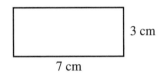

3 cm

7 cm

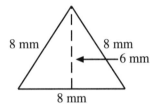

8 mm   8 mm
              6 mm

8 mm

5. perimeter _____

6. area _____

7. perimeter _____

8. area _____

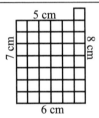

5 cm

7 cm   8 cm

6 cm

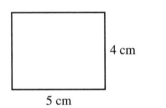

4 cm

5 cm

9. perimeter _____

10. area _____

11. perimeter _____

12. area _____

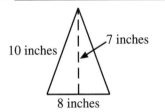

10 inches   7 inches

8 inches

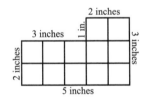

2 inches

3 inches   1 in.

2 inches   3 inches

5 inches

13. perimeter _____

14. area _____

15. perimeter _____

16. area _____

In the space below, draw a cube, a cone, and a pyramid.

Cube   Cone   Pyramid

World Landmarks. The answer for each world landmark trivia question is contained in the word search. Words may be written across, up, down, or diagonally.

Word Bank
Taj Mahal
Statue of Liberty
Great Pyramid at Giza
Parthenon
Angkor Wat
Tenochtitlan
Brasilia
Kremlin
Chichenitza
Vatican City
Great Wall of China
Stonehenge
CN Tower
Machu Picchu
Panama
Sydney Opera House

```
q p a n a m a x e j t a j m a h a l
s r l b a j u h s a u f o r x x n w
t o v e z n a l t i t h c o n e t b
g f q w e n o n e h t r a p x n b m
b v v a t i c a n c i t y t u c u h
q i n h q s o y r p i n i l m e r k
f e s u o h a r e p o y e n d y s a
g r e a t p y r a m i d a t g i z a
i q k l r s t o n e h e n g e w w f
n o b s t a t u e o f l i b e r t y
x v b m b d l c n t o w e r l f q i
m g r e a t w a l l o f c h i n a r
e l x u f b l s x t a w r o k g n a
y a z t i n e h c i h c n x p p v m
f u j n x u h c c i p u h c a m h j
m u z t r q k u i o a v e b i k z j
j w q p u x p s g y p k v o z d h g
u i f g b z x m m b r a s i l i a w
```

1. _____ was the capital of the Aztec Empire.

2. The "Green Lady" stands as a symbol of freedom in New York Harbor. _____

3. The _____ Canal is 50 miles long and 10 miles wide and connects the Atlantic and Pacific Oceans.

4. The ancient Inca city located in the Andes Mountains is _____.

5. _____ is the tallest free-standing structure in Canada.

6. _____ was a Mayan city built on Mexico's Yucatan Peninsula.

7. This South American national capital began construction in 1956 and is built in the shape of an airplane. _____

8. The world's smallest independent country is _____.

9. _____ is the most famous of Great Britain's stone rings.

10. _____ is the famous Greek temple dedicated to the goddess Athena.

11. This building is the center of Russian government. _____

12. The temple at the center of the Khmer Empire in Cambodia is _____.

13. This human-constructed structure is visible from space. _____

14. _____ is Australia's single most important architectural structure.

15. This Indian mausoleum is believed to be one of the most perfectly symmetric buildings in the world. _____

16. _____ is the tomb of the Pharaoh Cheops.

The Periodic Table. Do you know your symbols for the elements?

Which element does each symbol stand for?

Across

3. Cl
6. Ag
9. Ne
10. Ni
12. O
16. Ra
18. U
19. Na

Down

1. Kr
2. Pb
4. H
5. Hg
7. Fe
8. Ca
11. Cu
13. Au
14. He
15. K
17. Al

Word Bank

aluminum	helium	mercury	radon
calcium	hydrogen	neon	sodium
chlorine	iron	nickel	silver
copper	krypton	oxygen	uranium
gold	lead	potassium	

Library and Reference Materials. Answer the following questions about using the library and reference materials found in the library.

_____ 1. In which reference book would you look for general information? (It has multiple volumes and articles arranged alphabetically by subject.)
    A. general biographical reference   C. almanac
    B. atlas   D. encyclopedia

_____ 2. If you wanted to find information on a particular short story, in which source would you look?
    A. books of quotations   C. literary reference
    B. encyclopedia   D. newspaper

_____ 3. Suppose you were doing an inquiry paper or research paper on cloning. Which source would you use for up-to-date information?
    A. _Reader's Guide to Periodical Literature_   C. _Bartlett's Book of Quotations_
    B. _Compton's Encyclopedia_   D. _The International Who's Who_

_____ 4. If you were considering a vegetable garden this spring and you wanted to make sure you planted your peas and watermelons at the right time of the year, in which source would you look for such information?
    A. _National Geographic Atlas of the World_   C. _American Men and Women of Science_
    B. _The World Book Encyclopedia_   D. _The World Almanac and Book of Facts_

_____ 5. If you wanted to find a word or phrase that means the same as _somber_, in which source would you look?
    A. telephone directory   C. encyclopedia
    B. newspaper   D. thesaurus

_____ 6. In a book, where do you find the title, author, and publication information?
    A. table of contents   C. title page
    B. glossary   D. index

_____ 7. In which section of the newspaper would you find Help Wanted ads?
    A. front page   C. sports section
    B. entertainment section   D. classified section

_____ 8. Of the following words, which one would appear first in the dictionary?
    A. overshoe   C. overshadow
    B. overshot   D. overshoot

Positive and Negative Numbers.

Positive and negative numbers are also called *integers*. For every positive number there is an opposite, negative number. They are equidistant from 0 in the opposite directions on the number line. These numbers carry either the negative sign (-) or a positive sign (+). When a number appears with no sign, it is considered positive. Sometimes using a number line is helpful when working with integers.

Write the opposite term.

1. -3 _____   2. -14 _____   3. -10 _____   4. 30 _____

5. -2 _____   6. 89 _____   7. -56 _____   8. -165 _____

When adding or subtracting integers, it is important to pay attention to the signs.

9. -4 + 3 = _____   10. 5 + 9 = _____   11. 8 + (-10) = _____

12. -15 -7 = _____   13. 12 + (-7) = _____   14. 3 + (-8) = _____

15. (-10) + (-14) = _____   16. 2 + (-11) = _____   17. 6 - (-18) = _____

18. 7 + (-3) = _____   19. 6 + 8 = _____   20. 9 + (-13) = _____

21. (-14) + 5 = _____   22. 9 + (-8) = _____   23. -4 + 9 = _____

Using what you know about integers, solve the following by filling in the missing number.

24. -4 + ___ = 3   25. ___ - (8) = -18   26. -15 + ___ = -11

27. ___ - (-6) = 10   28. 20 + (-7) = ____   29. 16 + ___ = 12

Reading a Circle Graph. Using the circle graphs below, compare the religions of South Asia. A circle, or pie, graph is used to show the relationship between a whole and its parts. A whole circle stands for 100%, and pieces, or wedges, of the circle stand for percentages of the whole. Study the graphs below; then answer the questions that follow.

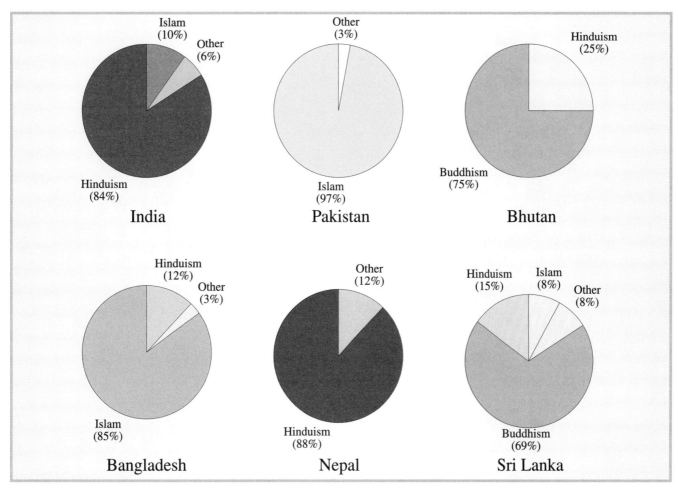

1. Followers of Islam make up 97% of the population of _____.

2. _____ has few or no Hindus.

3. The majority religion of Bhutan is _____.

4. Ten percent of the population of _____ are followers of Islam.

5. _____ has followers of all three major religions within its population.

6. The country with the highest percentage of people who follow Hinduism is _____.

7. The largest percentage of followers of other minority religions are in _____.

8. _____ has about an equal number of followers of Islam and other minority religions.

9. Which South Asian countries have more followers of Islam than any other religious groups? _____ and _____

Physical and Chemical Changes. Carbon dioxide is a colorless, odorless gas that does not support burning. Though you cannot see carbon dioxide, you can prove it is present. You can easily make carbon dioxide by mixing vinegar and baking soda.

candle   vinegar
small dish   glass
baking soda

1. Light a small candle; then use some of the wax from it to make the candle stand upright in a dish.

Note: Be sure one of your parents is present when you are doing this activity. Please be careful when you are working with matches and a lighted candle.

2. Pour a small amount of vinegar in a glass; then drop a small amount of baking soda into the vinegar. Now, notice what happens. What kind of change is this?

_____

3. Next, slowly tip the glass over the candle flame as if you were pouring something on the flame. Caution: Do not let any of the liquid pour onto the flame. What happens to the flame? Why?

_____

_____

_____

_____

Spelling. Read the following groups of words and choose the one that is spelled correctly.

____ 1. A. receeved
B. received
C. recieved
D. recieveed

____ 2. A. adorible
B. adoreable
C. adorable
D. adoorable

____ 3. A. principle of the school
B. prencipal of the school
C. principale of the school
D. principal of the school

____ 4. A. Its little feet are soft.
B. It's little feet are soft.
C. Its' little feet are soft.
D. Its's little feet are soft.

____ 5. A. Do you except this gift?
B. Do you acept this gift?
C. Do you accept this gift?
D. Do you ecept this gift?

____ 6. A. The desert was chocolate pie.
B. The dessert was chocolate pie.
C. The dassert was chocolate pie.
D. The dezert was chocolate pie.

____ 7. A. It was two quiet.
B. It was too's quiet.
C. It was to quiet.
D. It was too quiet.

____ 8. A. two deers in the woods
B. two deer in the woods
C. two deer's in the woods
D. two dear in the wooods

____ 9. A. Is this your book?
B. Is this you're book?
C. Is this yours book?
D. Is this yore book?

____10. A. They're books are lost.
B. There books are lost.
C. Their books are lost.
D. Theirs books are lost.

____11. A. Whose in charge?
B. Whose's in charge?
C. Whos' in charge?
D. Who's in charge?

____12. A. harmful gassis
B. harmful gases
C. harmful gasess'
D. harmful gassies

____13. A. a coarse of study
B. a course's of study
C. a course of study
D. a coarses of study

____14. A. happily
B. happyly
C. happilie
D. happile

____15. A. two radios
B. two radioos
C. two radioes
D. two radioess

____16. A. three brother-in-laws
B. three brothers-in-law
C. three brothers'-in-law
D. three brother's-in-law

Multiplying and Dividing Positive and Negative Numbers.

Multiplication:

Multiplying a negative number with a positive number gives a negative product.
Multiplying a positive number with a positive number gives a positive product.
Multiplying a negative number with a negative number gives a positive product.

Solve.

1. (-8) (9) = _____   2. 5 (-6) = _____   3. (-14) 2 = _____   4. (-2) 4 = _____

5. (9) (-4) = _____   6 (-7) (7) = _____   7. (-7) (-10) = _____   8. 9 (-8) = _____

9. (-3) (8) = _____   10. (5) (-5) = _____   11. 6 (-2) = _____   12. 11 (-2) = _____

13. (4) (-5) = _____   14. 4 (6) = _____   15. 9 (-12) = _____   16. 15 (-2) = _____

Division:

A positive number divided by a negative number gives a negative quotient.
A negative number divided by a positive number gives a negative quotient.
A positive number divided by a positive number gives a positive quotient.
A negative number divided by a negative number gives a positive quotient.

Solve.

17. 56 ÷ (-8) = _____   18. (45) ÷ (-5) = _____   19. (-14) ÷ 2 = _____

20. (-21) ÷ 3 = _____   21. -49 ÷ -7 = _____   22. 40 ÷ (-8) = _____

23. (-32) ÷ 8 = _____   24. 60 ÷ (-5) = _____   25. 72 ÷ (-8) = _____

26. If John gets on the elevator on the seventh floor and goes two floors up, then goes
    three floors down, and then rides two floors up again, what floor is he on now?

27. If Mary gets on the elevator in the basement and then goes three floors up and two
    floors down, which floor is she on now?

Need Help?
Check Out
Social Science Links at
www.summerbrains.com

Comparing Cultures. For each of the world regions listed, choose one country and research examples for each cell of the chart below. The Internet and your encyclopedia are two good sources of information for this activity.

Region	Anglo America	Latin America	Caribbean	Europe	Africa	Asia	Pacific
Country							
Food							
Language							
Religion							
Sports							
Leisure Activities							
Music							
Modes of Transportation							
Date of Independence							
Form of Government							

Atoms and Elements. The word *atom* comes from the Greek word *atomos* which means "indivisible." An atom is the smallest unit to which an element can be broken down. Atoms make up molecules, and molecules make up elements.

I. Answer these questions about the atom.

1. What is the atomic number? _____

2. What is the atomic mass? _____

3. What is the name of this element? _____

13 Protons

13 Neutrons

Electrons

II. Study the following word groups and eliminate the word that does not fit.

_____ 4. A. helium
          B. krypton
          C. neon
          D. oxygen

_____ 5. A. electrons
          B. isotopes
          C. protons
          D. neutrons

_____ 6. A. atom
          B. molecule
          C. subatomic particle
          D. element

_____ 7. A. Albert Einstein
          B. John Dalton
          C. Niels Bohr
          D. Ernest Rutherford

III. Write the letter of the best answer on the line to the left.

_____ 8. The elements on the left side of the periodic table tend to be
          A. active gases.   C. inactive gases.
          B. inactive solids.   D. active solids.

_____ 9. The elements on the right side of the periodic table tend to be
          A. active solids.   C. inactive solids.
          B. inactive gases.   D. active gases.

_____ 10. The element carbon
          A. is a metal.
          B. is found on the bottom of the periodic table.
          C. is found on the far right of the periodic table.
          D. forms organic compounds.

Vocabulary. Use context clues to find the *synonyms* for the underlined words.

____ 1. Even though the little dog seemed <u>docile</u>, its eyes followed us in the room.
    A. frightened   C. nervous
    B. calm   D. happy

____ 2. The yearbook staff hopes to include many <u>candid</u> shots of students around school.
    A. hidden   C. athletic
    B. sarcastic   D. unposed

____ 3. I don't like selling magazine subscriptions door to door all day because it is such a <u>grueling</u> ordeal.
    A. exhausting   C. enjoyable
    B. difficult   D. time consuming

____ 4. The black clouds looked <u>ominous</u> as we kept driving.
    A. boring   C. threatening
    B. satisfied   D. rainy

____ 5. It would be a <u>fallacy</u> to think that a rabid dog can't harm anyone or anything.
    A. sign   C. threat
    B. mistake   D. problem

____ 6. The <u>frenzied</u> sports fans pushed down the gate and burst into the stadium.
    A. happy   C. ethnic
    B. mixed   D. excited

____ 7. She was <u>ostracized</u> from the town and had to live on the outskirts.
    A. banished   C. appointed
    B. punished   D. elected

____ 8. His teacher always brags that he is responsible and <u>competent</u>.
    A. unhappy   C. hungry
    B. mischievous   D. skillful

Prefixes and Roots. In the blanks provided, write the meaning of the following.

____ 9. ad-   ____13. -cid-   ____17. tri-
____10. intra-   ____14. auto-   ____18. geo-
____11. sub-   ____15. micro-   ____19. -phon-
____12. re-   ____16. -pod   ____20. -dic-

Square Roots and Exponents.

Find the square root of each number given below.

1. 25 = _____   2. 16 = _____   3. 49 = _____   4. 121 = _____

5. 1,681 = _____   6. 1,296 = _____   7. 625 = _____   8. 81 = _____

9. 256 = _____   10. 100 = _____   11. 324 = _____   12. 144 =_____

Write the number, using exponents, represented by each expression.

13. 2 x 2 x 2 x 2 x 2 = _____   14. 5 x 5 x 5 x 5 = _____

15. 7 x 7 x 7 x 7 x 7 x 7 = _____   16. 8 x 8 x 8 = _____

17. 10 x 10 x 10 x 10 = _____   18. 3 x 3 x 3 x 3 x 3 = _____

Compare using <, >, or =.

19. 4^3_____81   20. 5^5_____20   21. 7^3_____343

22. 8^2_____ 98   23. 449 _____ 4^9 24. 81 _____10^3

Creating a Word Search.

Choose 20 words that relate to your state, territory, or province and its citizens. List the words alphabetically on the lines below. Next, write each word, letter by letter, in the graph below. Write the words up and down, side to side, or diagonally. Fill in all of the remaining squares with "junk" letters. Give the word search to a friend to solve.

_____   _____   _____   _____

_____   _____   _____   _____

_____   _____   _____   _____

_____   _____   _____   _____

_____   _____   _____   _____

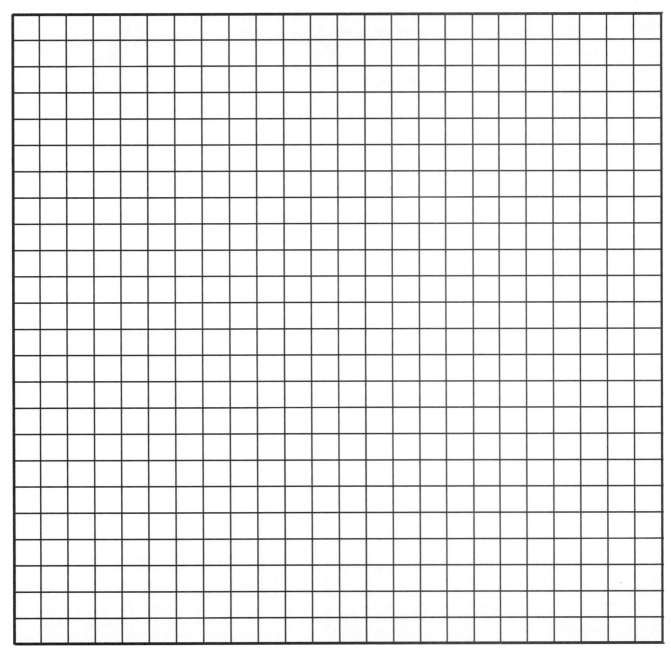

The Ear. The ear is an organ in our body that detects sound. Three things are needed for sounds to be heard: (1) a source that produces the sound, (2) a medium to transmit the sound, and (3) an organ that detects the sound. Identify the parts of the ear by placing the number beside the name.

hammer

anvil

stirrup

external auditory canal

vestibular nerve

bones

cochlea

cochlear nerve

eardrum

eustachian tube

semicircular canals

auricle

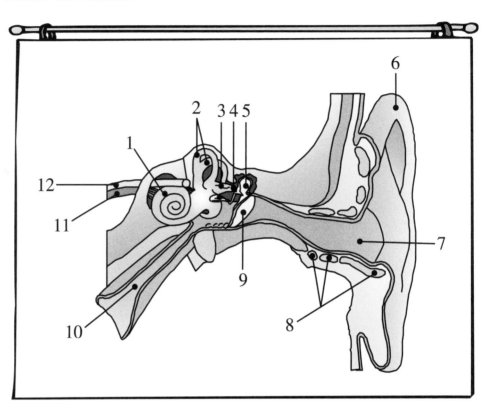

True or False. If the following statements are true, write T; if false, write F.

_____ 1. The stirrup is part of the middle ear.

_____ 2. The loudness of a sound depends on its amplitude.

_____ 3. An example of a percussion instrument is a trumpet.

_____ 4. The speed of sound increases with increasing temperature.

_____ 5. Materials that transmit sound easily are nonelastic.

_____ 6. The speed of sound in air is approximately 340 m/sec.

_____ 7. The loudness of a sound is called its intensity.

_____ 8. Sound greater than 120 decibels can cause pain in humans.

_____ 9. The part of the ear that is set into vibration by vibrating air molecules is the cochlea.

_____ 10. The funnel for sound waves in the ear is the outer ear.

An *informative paragraph* is one that gives information on a particular topic of interest. Facts and statistics are useful for developing these paragraphs that give information. In gathering facts and statistics, use reliable sources, such as publications and Internet sites from reputable organizations, encyclopedias, experts, etc. As you select details to use, keep your readers in mind. Don't give too much information, so your readers don't become bored or confused. Arrange your material in an order that will be easy to follow. Don't forget to include a *topic sentence* that states your main idea or purpose. In the lines provided below, write an *informative paragraph* on some topic that interests you and will interest your readers.

_____

_____

_____

_____

_____

_____

_____

_____

_____

_____

_____

_____

_____

_____

Prefixes and Roots. In the lines below, write what the following mean.

_____ 1. -tract-   _____ 5. -cis-

_____ 2. -phobia-   _____ 6. bi-

_____ 3. eu-   _____ 7. -fid-

_____ 4. con-   _____ 8. -graph-

Spelling. In the word groups below, choose the word that is misspelled.

_____ 9. A. seperate   _____ 10. A. committee   _____ 11. A. forty
         B. scissors   B. condemm   B. definition
         C. sense   C. conscience   C. governer
         D. surprise   D. conceive   D. describe

Problem Solving.

Use what you know to solve these problems. In some cases a picture or number line may help. Also use the previous pages for reference.

1. A compact disc costs $11.95. How much do four of them cost if they are on sale for 10% off the original price?

2. A pound of apples costs 85¢. How much would four and one-half pounds cost?

3. Mr. Jones grilled a steak that weighed 1.9 kg before it was cooked. After it was grilled, it weighed 1.1 kg. How much weight did the steak lose while cooking?

4. Mrs. Adams wants to fill a 2.5 liter jug with lemonade. She has made 1.5 liters. How much more lemonade should she make to fill the jug?

5. Three students in Mrs. Moore's class brought pizza for the class. One pizza had one-eighth left, another had three-fifths left, and the last pizza had one-tenth left over. How much pizza was left in all?

6. Marc likes to keep up with his grades in science. He made two 100s on tests, and on his other two tests he scored 87 and 97. What is his average test grade?

7. Corey likes to swim laps in gym. If she swims 4.5 meters one day, 7.8 the next, and 5.3 meters the third day, what is her total for the week at this point?

8. Melanie bought a new stereo system for $1,500.00. She was able to put it on her credit card and pay on it monthly. If her annual interest rate is 7% and she has the debt for two years, how much interest will she have to pay?

9. Gina wants to increase her savings account. She started with $400.00. Then she deposited $75.00 in it one week. The following week she had to withdraw $125.00 to pay for car repairs. What is her balance now?

10. Susan is a veterinarian. If she sees one bird, twelve dogs, and seven cats in one day and charges $65.00 per animal, what are her total charges for office services that day?

Incentive Contract Calendar

Month _____

My parents and I decided that if I complete 15 days of
Summer Bridge Activities™ 7–8 and read _____ minutes a day,
my incentive/reward will be:

_____

Child's Signature_____

Parent's Signature_____

EXAMPLE: ✔ ✔ _AC_

Day 1 ☐ ☐ ____
Day 2 ☐ ☐ ____
Day 3 ☐ ☐ ____
Day 4 ☐ ☐ ____
Day 5 ☐ ☐ ____
Day 6 ☐ ☐ ____
Day 7 ☐ ☐ ____

Day 8 ☐ ☐ ____
Day 9 ☐ ☐ ____
Day 10 ☐ ☐ ____
Day 11 ☐ ☐ ____
Day 12 ☐ ☐ ____
Day 13 ☐ ☐ ____
Day 14 ☐ ☐ ____
Day 15 ☐ ☐ ____

Child: Put a ✔ in the ☐ for the daily activities ▱ completed.

Put a ✔ in the ☐ for the daily reading ▰ completed.

Parent: Initial the ____ for daily activities and reading your child completes.

Get Ready for Back to School

Shopping List

What classes will you need to take to get your dream job?

Where do you want to work?

Things to Do

Class Schedule

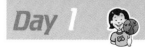

Creating a Map. On this page sketch the outline of your state, province, or territory. Locate and label the capital, your hometown, and important physical, political, and historical places. Use colored pencils to make the map more interesting.

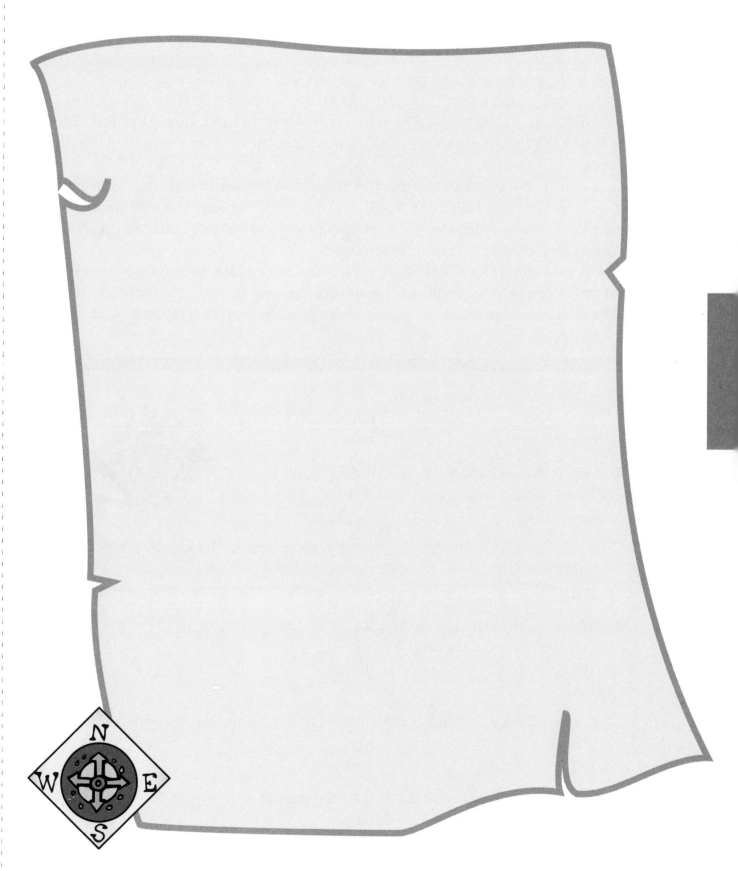

Reading Comprehension. Answer the questions below after reading the passage.

The Eye

Your eye is nature's own camera. Your eyes act very similarly to an ordinary camera. Furthermore, your eyes are linked to your brain similar to the way a television camera is connected to its transmitter.

Light enters the eye through a tough transparent skin called the cornea, where the light is partially bent, or refracted. Then the light enters through a flexible convex lens which focuses the light on the retina. The retina is sensitive to light, much like the film of the camera. When the light strikes the retina, electric impulses follow the optic nerve to the visual center of the brain.

There is a part in the eye that controls the amount of light that can enter your eye. It is a colored, constricting ring called the iris. It is just outside the lens and acts similarly to the diaphragm of a camera. Likewise, your eyelids correspond to the shutter of the camera, which opens and closes to expose the film.

The lens of your eye is flexible. The lens can bulge out or flatten to focus on objects that are near or far away. To focus on nearby objects, muscles in your eye cause the lens to bulge out. The lens muscles are usually relaxed when focusing on objects twenty or more feet away.

_____ 1. Light enters the eye through the
    A. iris.   C. cornea.
    B. convex lens.   D. retina.

_____ 2. The iris is similar to the _____ of the camera.
    A. lens   C. shutter
    B. transmitter   D. diaphragm

_____ 3. To focus on nearby objects, _____ in your eye cause the lens to bulge.
    A. shutters   C. nerves
    B. muscles   D. optic nerve

_____ 4. After the light enters the cornea, it is bent and goes through the convex lens, which focuses the light on the _____.
    A. retina   C. muscles
    B. iris   D. optic nerve

_____ 5. This part of the eye controls the amount of light that can enter the eye.
    A. cornea   C. iris
    B. retina   D. lens

_____ 6. What part of your eye corresponds to the shutter of a camera?
    A. iris   C. retina
    B. cornea   D. eyelids

Just for Fun Crossword Puzzle. Examine the list of words in the Word Bank, and then, using the clues below, solve the crossword puzzle.

Word Bank

noun
pronoun
adjective
adverb
conjunction
preposition
interjection
sentence
fragment
homophone
clause
possessive
phrase
comma
dependent

Across

2. a group of words that expresses a complete thought

3. a group of words that does not contain a subject and verb

6. a word that takes the place of a person, place, or thing

8. a clause that cannot stand alone

9. a punctuation mark used to separate words or groups of words

12. a word that joins words or groups of words

13. a word that shows ownership

14. a word that shows a relationship between a noun or pronoun and another word in a sentence

15. a group of words that contains a subject and a verb

Down

1. a word that shows strong feeling

4. a word that describes a verb, adjective, or adverb

5. a word that names a person, place, or thing.

7. a word that describes a noun or pronoun

10. a group of words that does not express a complete thought

11. words that sound alike but have different meanings

Evaluating Expressions.

Expressions are mathematical ways to represent a quantity. Often the values of the variables will be given, and the expression can be simplified by merely substituting the values for each variable.

You can solve the following by substituting the values given for each variable.

If: $a = 5$ $b = 3$ $c = 8$

1. $4b =$ _____

2. $6 + c =$ _____

3. $a(7 + 5) =$ _____

4. $b(7 + 3) =$ _____

5. $7b + 8c =$ _____

6. $(9 + 9) \div b =$ _____

7. $ab + (7 - 12) =$ _____

8. $(4 + 9)(b + 3) =$ _____

9. $c(7 + 5) + (7 + 3) =$ _____

10. $7ca =$ _____

11. $(10 \div a) + (b + 2) =$ _____

12. $3(a + c) =$ _____

13. $5a + 7c =$ _____

Problem Solving.

Example: 2 times a number plus 2 = <u>$2n + 2$</u>

Write an algebraic sentence to illustrate the phrases using variables.

14. 7 less than a number _____

15. 2 more than 3 times a number _____

16. the product of 9 and a number decreased by 8 _____

17. the difference between a number and 5 _____

18. the sum of a number and 4 _____

19. 5 times a number plus 6 times the same number _____

20. a number divided by 12 _____

Local Trivia. Locate and list the following trivia for your state, province, or territory.

Postal Code: _____

Nickname: _____

Motto: _____

Song: _____

Bird: _____

Tree: _____

Flower: _____

Time Zone(s): _____

Historical Event(s): _____

Historical Hero: _____

Famous Person(s): _____

Governor: _____

Capital: _____

Population: _____

Tourist Attraction: _____

Largest City: _____

Natural Resources: _____

First Inhabitants: _____

Principal Industry: _____

Principal Agricultural Crop: _____

Natural Wonder: _____

Mineral Resources: _____

Highest Point: _____

Lowest Point: _____

Monument(s): _____

The Eye. The eye is an organ that allows us to see light through a series of steps that involve the various parts of the eye and the brain. Label the parts of the eye.

retina
cornea
iris
lens
optic nerve
pupil
vitreous humor

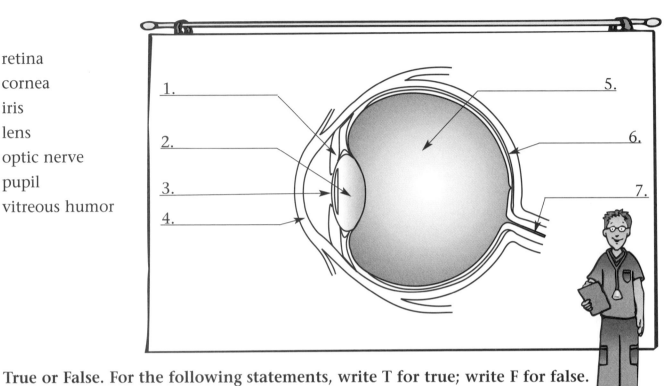

True or False. For the following statements, write T for true; write F for false.

____ 1. The moon is an example of an illuminated object.

____ 2. Light waves are electric and magnetic.

____ 3. Light is composed of a stream of energy clusters called photons.

____ 4. The speed of light is fastest in a liquid.

____ 5. Ordinary lightbulbs provide fluorescent light.

____ 6. A candle flame is seen because it is luminous.

____ 7. Infrared rays can be seen.

____ 8. The moon is a luminous object.

____ 9. Red light can be produced by neon gas.

____10. The speed of light in a vacuum is 300,000 km/sec.

Fill in the blanks using the following words: *book, ultraviolet, light, photon, incandescent.*

11. A _____ is a bundle of light energy.

12. _____ rays are responsible for vitamin D production and tanning.

13. _____ can be transmitted with or without a medium.

14. A _____ is an example of an illuminated object.

15. _____ light is produced from heat.

Transitive and Intransitive Verbs. A *transitive verb* has an object, and an *intransitive verb* does not have an object. In the sentences below, write the verb in the blank, and indicate if the verb is transitive (tr.) or intransitive (intr.).

_____ 1. We drifted all day on the river.

_____ 2. Jeff drove the car to the store while his dad repaired the van.

_____ 3. Lisa wrote carefully, thinking about every word.

_____ 4. During lunch Grayson wrote a poem for the class to read.

_____ 5. The package was delivered early Saturday to Jack's house on the river near the swinging bridge.

_____ 6. Last summer Josh and Wes hiked the Appalachian Mountains.

need help?
Check Out
Grammar Links at
www.summerbrains.com

A *linking verb* is a verb that serves as a link between two words. The link is between the noun or pronoun before the verb and the noun, pronoun, or adjective that follows the verb. In the sentences below, identify the linking verbs, and then give the words that are linked by the verbs.

7. This is the new performing arts building._____

8. His new red car looks good. _____

9. We waited so long for our meal that anything would have tasted delicious._____

10. The baby kitten was so small. _____

11. When Jesse walked into the classroom last, he felt embarrassed. _____

12. Zac is president of his class again. _____

13. He is Sam. _____

14. After playing a hard game for two hours, Seth looked tired but happy. _____

15. The moose ran for five minutes and then was out of sight. _____

16. The engineer sounded his horn, and the train actually looked upset. _____

17. This is she._____

18. Jennifer is going to the prom with Joseph. _____

Multiplication and Division with Rational Numbers.

A ratio is a quotient of a number, like $\frac{8}{4} = 2$. Rational expressions are simplified by combining like terms and following the order of operations (see page 115).

Simplify the following.

1. $-36 \div 6 + 2\frac{1}{3}$

2. $-9 \div -3 + 4(-\frac{1}{4}) - 20 \div 5$

3. $\frac{12 - 2}{5} = c$

4. $-\frac{3}{8}(-4) = q$

5. $\frac{1}{3}[(-18 + 3) + (5 + 7) \div -4]$

6. $\frac{60 \times \frac{1}{2}}{-10 + 15} + 35$

7. $2[-6(3 - 12) - 17]$

8. $\frac{1}{4}(20 + 72 \div 9)$

9. $\frac{1}{2}(-18 - 2)$

10. $2(3 - 15) + 5$

Compare the following rational numbers using <, >, or =.

11. 2.5 _____ $2\frac{18}{36}$

12. -3.0 _____ -0.3

13. $-7\frac{1}{5}$ _____ $-7\frac{5}{25}$

14. 37.56 _____ 365.6

15. 15.63 _____ 1.563

16. 8.30 _____ -8.30

Draw the flag of your state, province, or territory. Be sure to color the flag accurately. Explain its significance.

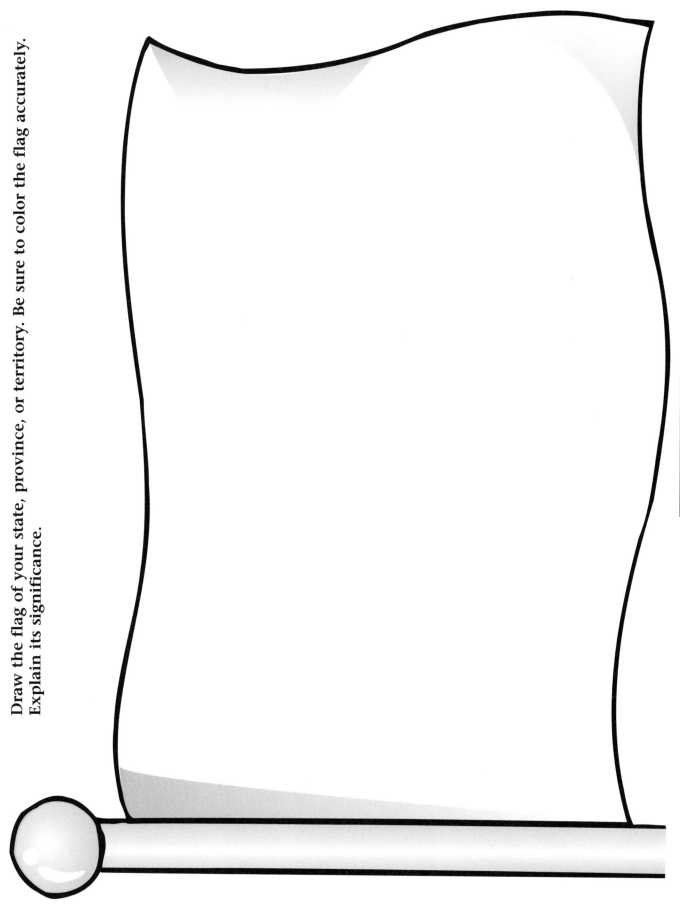

Them Bones, Them Bones! Can you locate all the bones on the crossword puzzle?

Word Bank

calcaneus
carpus
clavicle
coccyx
fibula
humerus
mandible
patella
phalanges
radius
scapula
sternum
tarsus
tibia
ulna

Clues

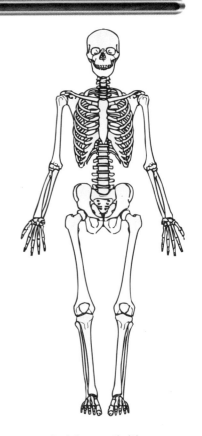

Down

1. the heel bone
2. the ankle bone
4. bones between two joints (i.e., fingers)
6. the shinbone
7. the upper arm bone
8. the collarbone
11. the tailbone
12. the shorter forearm bone
13. the larger forearm bone

Across

3. the thigh bone
5. the breastbone
9. lower jaw bone
10. the kneecap
11. the wrist bone
14. the shoulder bone

Appositives. An *appositive* is a noun or pronoun that follows another noun or pronoun and identifies or explains it. In the following sentences, check for errors in the use of commas and appositives or appositive phrases. On the line, write the word(s) before a comma is needed. If the sentence is correct, write C.

_____ 1. Toni the new girl from Italy is a good student.

_____ 2. The new girl Toni came from Italy.

_____ 3. The club members who have paid their dues can go to the picnic.

_____ 4. My friend Ben is writing a story about Chicago his favorite place in the world.

_____ 5. Vanessa the superstar athlete is giving a speech tomorrow night in the middle school's auditorium.

_____ 6. Did you read *The Giver* a book about what the future might be like?

_____ 7. Her longtime friend and correspondent Beth McCoy will be here on Saturday morning to help with the long move to the East.

Pronoun Agreement. Read the sentences below, and on the lines provided write the correct pronoun.

_____ 8. Each of the girls rode (her, their) bicycle to school.

_____ 9. One of the men in the drama class designed (his, their) own costume.

_____ 10. A person should always try (his, her, his or her, their) best.

_____ 11. Angela and Grayson left late because (they, she) had to do some extra work.

_____ 12. Neither Dana nor Lynn saw (herself, themselves) in the class portrait.

_____ 13. Someone else in our class has also submitted (his or her, their) own request to get the grant money.

_____ 14. Each boy bowed politely, saying that (he, they) would do (his, their) share of the project.

_____ 15. Anyone can go if (he, she, he or she, they) has paid for the ticket into the park.

_____ 16. The two boys baked the cake (theirselves, themselves).

_____ 17. Anyone can see that it is best to do (one's, their) own work, instead of copying someone else's work.

Day 6

Polynomials.   2-5-07

NEED HELP?
Check Out
Math Links at
www.summerbrains.com

Combine the like terms.

1. 11ab + 12ab + 6ab

    29ab

2. 4y – 9y – 3y

3. 5x + 3ax – 2ax

    60x

4. 9ay + 10x – 4ay

5. 6a + 12a

    18a

6. 4b + 3c – 6b + 2 + 3b

7. 4cd – 12cd

    -8cd

8. -16x + 8x + 4

9. -8xy + 10xy – 3b

    2xy - 3b

10. 6 – 2a + 3a – 5

11. 8x + (2x – 5)

    10x - 5

12. (5x + 3y + p)

13. 3a – (2b – 3c)

    3a - 2b - 3c

14. (7x – y) + 32

15. -(ax – 3bx) + 4x

16. 7x – 3a – (4b)

17. 5n – (8a + 2b)

18. 3x – (5y + 4y)

19. (2bx – 4bx) + 4x

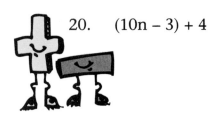

20. (10n – 3) + 4

Creating a Timeline. Create a timeline for your state, province, or territory. Begin with its earliest inhabitants and continue to the present.

Start

Today

Time Machine

The Digestive System. In digestion, complex foods are broken down into smaller molecules of water soluble substances that can be used by the body's cells. The first part of the change that occurs during digestion is mechanical. This phase involves chewing and the constant churning and mixing action brought about by the muscular movement of the walls of the digestive organs. The breakdown of food into small particles and thorough mixing with various juices aids the second phase of digestion, which is chemical.

I. Using the numbered items, identify the parts of the digestive system.

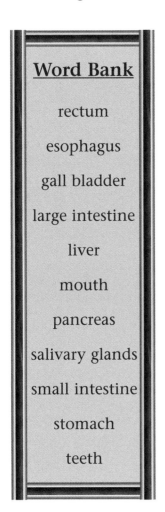

Word Bank

rectum

esophagus

gall bladder

large intestine

liver

mouth

pancreas

salivary glands

small intestine

stomach

teeth

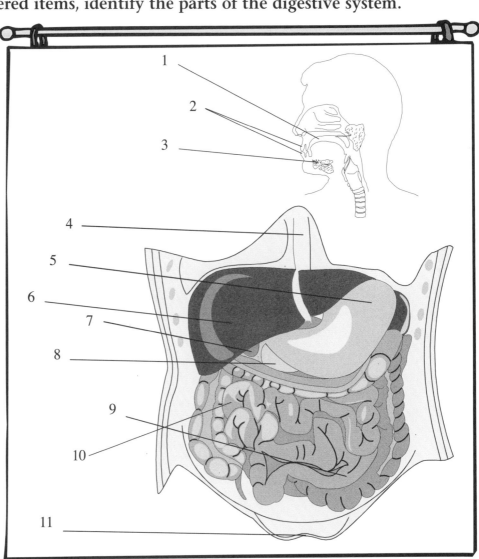

II. Digestive Trivia. Fill in the blanks for the following questions.

1. What is the function of the appendix? _____

2. How long does the digestive process take? _____

3. Which is the largest internal organ? _____

4. What is the largest gland in the body? _____

5. Name the four types of teeth found in humans. _____

6. What is the structure that keeps food from going down the windpipe? _____

Vocabulary and Context Clues. Read the following sentences, and choose a word that means the *opposite* of the underlined words.

_____ 1. The <u>upholding</u> of this law in the state became a farce.
     A. undermining   C. trial
     B. model   D. scene

_____ 2. Shantel never thinks of the <u>orthodox</u> way to solve her problems.
     A. conventional   C. unconventional
     B. right   D. wrong

_____ 3. Joshua, like his baseball teammates, was <u>exultant</u> over the win against Idaho Falls.
     A. sad   C. sick
     B. happy   D. healthy

_____ 4. The weather was <u>balmy</u> this morning, but this afternoon it looks stormy.
     A. calm   C. warm
     B. pleasant   D. violent

_____ 5. Last night the coach encouraged the golf team instead of <u>demoralizing</u> them after the loss.
     A. insulting   C. encouraging
     B. cursing   D. fighting

Homophones are words that are spelled differently but sound the same. In the following sentences, choose the correct words, and place them on the line provided.

_____ 6. His commander said he would never (desert, dessert) his post.

_____ 7. Did you (hear, here) the good news, Ashley?

_____ 8. Even though he (led, lead) us through the dark woods, I still didn't totally trust the strange-looking man with the dog.

_____ 9. A (piece, peace) treaty was signed by the Native Americans on this riverbank.

_____ 10. If you decide to write the letter, use the gray (stationary, stationery).

_____ 11. (They're, There, Their) are people swimming in the lake right now.

_____ 12. This is not (quiet, quite) what I had in mind for a science project.

_____ 13. It is (to, too, two) late (to, too, two) go (to, too, two) the park.

Solving Equations.

An equation is an algebraic algorithm that is used to solve for an unknown value or variable. There is an equals (=) sign in an equation. There is not one in an expression; therefore, equations may be solved, not just simplified. Answers could be whole numbers, negative numbers, or rational numbers.

Example:

5y + 6 = 2y + 15 (The 2y will be subtracted from both sides.)
3y + 6 = 15 (Next, the 6 will be subtracted from both sides.)
3y = 9 (The 3 will be divided into the numbers on each side.)
Thus: y = 3

Solve the following equations. Round to the nearest hundredth if necessary.

1. 3x + 1 = 15

2. -2 + 4x = 13

3. 8x + (-4) = 12

4. 9 + 4x = 45

5. 8x – (2 + 3) = 11

6. 7x + 2 – 3x = 18

7. 12 + 3x – 9x = -18

8. (6x + 2) + 7x = 41

9. (6x) – (2x) = 40

10. (8x + 3) + (4x + 2) = 17

11. 14x + 3 = -4x – 6

12. -180 = 12b

13. 42 = -14p

14. 75 = -5(a + 5)

15. 63 = 9(2 – a)

16. -54 = 3(2 + 5m)

17. 17(x – 2) = -34

18. -x – 15 = -15

Physical Geography. Trace or sketch the outline of your state, province, or territory. Sketch in and label each geographic region (coastal plain, piedmont, upland, etc.). You may choose to color each region a different color. Sketch in and label the major physical features (rivers, mountains, lakes, swamps, oceans, etc.).

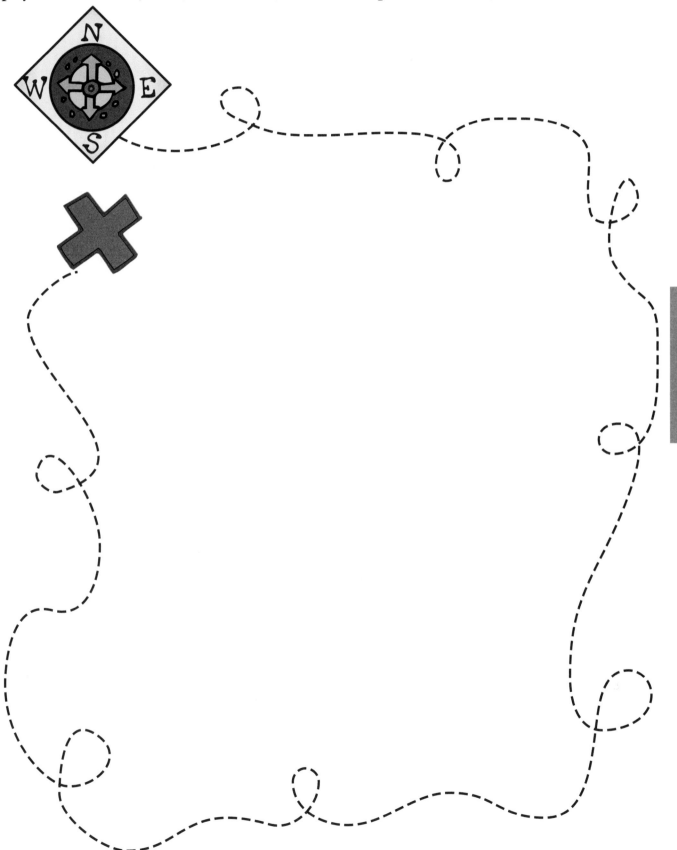

Cells. The tiny cell is the basic building block in all living things. There are two basic types of cells: animal and plant cells.

Are you confused about cells? Well, don't be! Find the 20 words that are related to cells.

```
o f q b m i t o c h o n d r i a c g l a
i m u k a t u d v a c u o l e c z k c e
d a q w o i f e m o s o s y l r k g f n
t t m x r c c h r o m o s o m e s j t a
z v q o g h k m z t s n u c l e u s f r
c t w i a l a d a l d e n n s o y j i b
y e d o n o w u l x i r d u d r v x h m
t o r s r r a e o i c b j c n g a f q e
o m l k n o c l f g a w u l a a z v o m
p p k y l p q s g f c w v e o n w b p l
l g j a l l r u d w i l m a v i f a g l
a j l u a a i l z a e t x r b s p u o e
s j c q w s b o s s l i e m t m l f d c
m a o u l t o e q m c s a e y o w a f n
y i w g l e s l q r u s v m e j j u v c
s h h j e b o c y x n u z b n u m v l v
x b m n c s m u a q o e c r h k f y w u
z y r f i v e n w r o r g a n e l l e s
l q n r h a j s u g r c f n b z o w h l
g p a o t t m z e u s v z e h f x g p a
```

Word Bank

nucleus	mitochondria	nucleolus	DNA
cell membrane	nucleic acids	cell	organelles
cell wall	lysosome	organism	RNA
nuclear membrane	chloroplast	tissue	organ
ribosome	vacuole	chromosomes	cytoplasm

A *sentence fragment* is part of a sentence. It is not a complete sentence, even though the fragment may be punctuated as if it were a sentence. Read the following word groups, and if the group is a fragment write F on the line. If the group is a sentence, write S on the line.

_____ 1. When they took the SAT last April.

_____ 2. Because everyone at school was required to take the test and hopefully do well.

_____ 3. Did everyone bring a pencil to use on the test?

_____ 4. Take your time.

_____ 5. Denise on this test when she took it in 1998.

_____ 6. After all the students had left the classroom, the testing administrator gave a sigh of relief.

_____ 7. Do the best you can.

_____ 8. Raising her hand and asking for permission to sharpen her pencil before the test began.

_____ 9. The SAT is something we do every spring at my school in Tennessee.

_____ 10. Gave the directions and asked everyone to remain quiet after the test.

A *run-on sentence* is a sentence in which two or more sentences are run together, as if they were one. Two ways a run-on sentence can be corrected are (1) by using a period to separate the sentences, or (2) using a comma and a coordinating conjunction such as *and*, *but*, or *or* between the sentences. If the following groups of words are run-ons, revise them. If the group of words is correct, write C on the line.

_____ 11. Our school is the largest in the county, it is also one of the oldest.

_____ 12. The rooms are carpeted and well-lighted also each room has sturdy desks.

_____ 13. When the new school opened, all the students were given a party on the lawn.

_____ 14. The new school already has a student population of 1,200, it only has a capacity for 1,250 students.

_____ 15. The students are excited about the new school they are taking precautions to keep the school clean for everyone to enjoy.

_____ 16. Since the opening, our new school has received much publicity.

_____ 17. Our principal has been friendlier since the school opened everyone likes him.

Polynomials.

Use the vertical format to combine the like terms and simplify each polynomial.
Remember to change the positive and negative signs when you subtract!

Example:

1.   7ax + 4a
    + (3ax – a)
    10ax + 3a

2.   -4x + 3y
    + (-5x – 10y)

3.   12ab – 12q
    – (3ab + 6q)

4.   2x – 18
    – (-3x – 9)

5.   -7y – 4z
    + 18y – 12z

6.   9x – 5
    + (-4x + 10)

7.   11ab + 4c
    + (-12ab – 5c)

8.   -2ay + 3y
    – (-6ay – 4y)

9.   -3a – 4b
    – (6a + 5b)

10.   -8b – 3
    – (-10b – 4)

11.   -7n + 3
    – (-7n + 3)

12.   7y + 3z
    – (-6y – 2z)

13.   -4b – 3c
    – (5b – 6c)

14.   3ab – 6c
    + (4ab + 3c)

15.   16y + 3b
    – (14y + 7b)

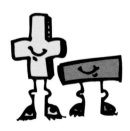

Your State, Province, or Territory "Ologies." For each category below, research specifics related to the subject and your area.

Anthropology _____

_____

_____

Archaeology _____

_____

_____

Biology (flora) _____

_____

_____

Ecology _____

_____

_____

Entomology _____

_____

_____

Geology _____

_____

_____

Ichthyology _____

_____

_____

Ornithology _____

_____

_____

Zoology _____

_____

_____

Photosynthesis. *Photosynthesis* is defined as the process by which certain living plant cells combine carbon dioxide and water in the presence of chlorophyll and light energy to form carbohydrates and release oxygen as a waste product. The name nearly defines the process, for *photo* refers to light, while *synthesis* means the building of a complex substance from simple substances.

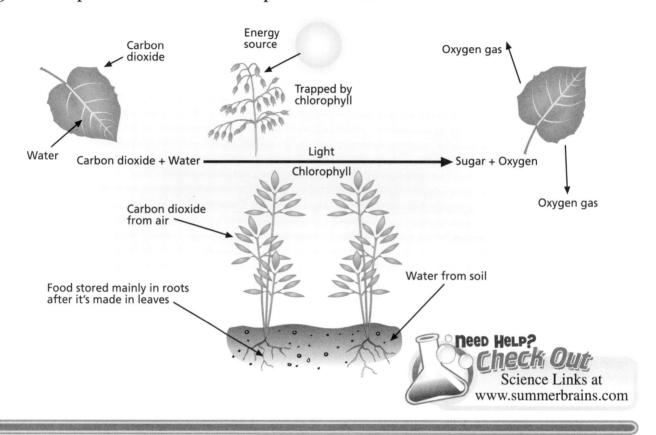

Respond to the following questions on photosynthesis. If you need assistance, use a reference or biology book.

1. In order for photosynthesis to take place in plants, how do they get the carbon dioxide they need?

   _____

2. What is the function of photosynthesis?

   _____

3. During photosynthesis what happens to the oxygen that is produced?

   _____

4. Where do plants get the energy necessary for the chemical reactions that take place during photosynthesis? _____

A *double comparison* is the use of both *-er* and *more* (*less*) or both *-est* and *most* (*least*) in a comparison. For example, you don't say that your sister is a more better basketball player than you are. Revise the following sentences by putting an X through any unneeded words. Then place the correct forms on the lines. If a sentence is correct, write C.

_____ 1. The most biggest watermelon I have ever seen was grown by my grandfather.

_____ 2. Your voice sounds worser today.

_____ 3. After watching the two swimmers for fifteen minutes, we finally chose the most aggressive one.

_____ 4. Is Jupiter larger than any planet in the solar system?

_____ 5. She gets to wear the beautifulest clothes of anyone I know.

_____ 6. This paint is more whiter than that one on the second shelf.

_____ 7. He was the most talented actor in the group, according to everyone on stage.

_____ 8. Tanner likes the ham sandwiches more better than the roast beef sandwiches.

_____ 9. Of the three children, Grayson is the tallest and the oldest.

A *double negative* is the use of two negative words to express one negative idea. Revise the following sentences, eliminating the double negatives. Draw an X through the incorrect word, and write the new word on the line. If the sentence is correct, write C on the line.

_____ 10. Terry hasn't never been to Sweden.

_____ 11. Although Tonya never had no problems with poetry, she is having some difficulty with writing essays.

_____ 12. The math winner doesn't have no excuse.

_____ 13. He was so excited he couldn't hardly talk.

_____ 14. The principal doesn't allow no students at school after 4:00.

_____ 15. Tim never listens to no one who argues.

_____ 16. Don't never say *not*.

_____ 17. She didn't have nothing left for herself.

_____ 18. I am never going to see that sad movie again.

Graphing.

The Cartesian coordinate system is a system of two perpendicular number lines intersecting at the point zero, which is called the origin. This forms a grid with four quadrants. The horizontal line is called the x-axis, and the vertical line is the y-axis. This graph is used for plotting points, solving systems of equations, and other uses you will learn later in algebra.

Use the Cartesian coordinate system to plot the following points:

1. (-2, 3)	2. (0, 0)	3. (2, -7)	4. (5, -1)
5. (9, 8)	6. (-4, -4)	7. (5, 8)	8. (-3, -8)
9. (5, -9)	10. (-1, 2)	11. (0, -10)	12. (7, -6)

13. On the graph use a straight edge to connect three points in the three possible lines.

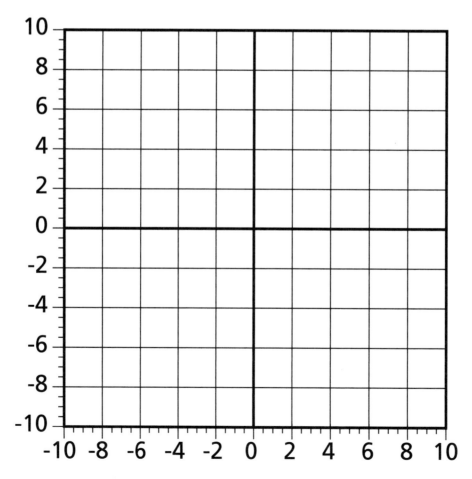

The Place I Call Home

Create a scrapbook of your community. Be sure to include the complete name, location, date of founding, and history of the area. Who were some of the famous and/or important native sons and daughters? For what is your community famous? What products, goods, and services are produced in your area? Create a map that includes landmarks and geological features. Collect pictures, drawings, and illustrations. You may choose to include pages on food, music, festivals, and special events.

Use the space below to begin brainstorming and note-taking. Be sure to tap different resources: the library, town hall, local officials, friends, family, web sites, various information programs, and CDs.

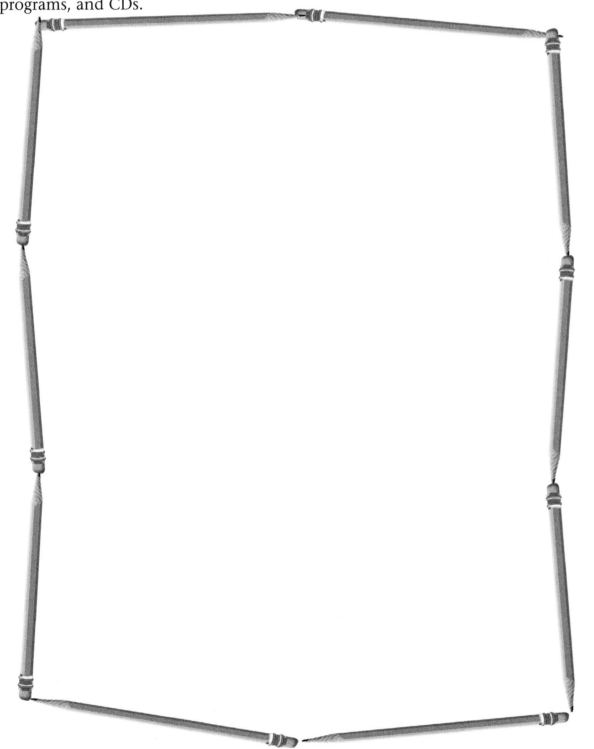

Genetics. *Genetics* is the study of heredity, or the passing on of traits from an organism to its offspring. Probability can be used to predict the results of genetic combinations. In addition to probability, a chart called a Punnett Square can be used to show the possible gene combinations in a cross between two organisms. *Phenotype* refers to physical appearance, and *genotype* refers to the actual gene make-up.

Situation 1. Suppose you have two mice, one black and one white. The genotype for the black mouse is WW, and the genotype for the white mouse is ww. As you note, W is dominant, and w is recessive. In the Punnett Square below, cross the two parents and fill in the possible gene combinations for the offspring.

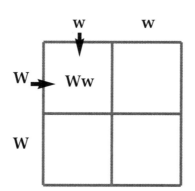

Situation 2. Take two of the offspring in Situation 1 and cross them in this Punnett Square.

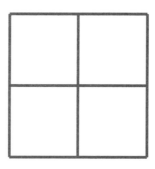

1. If you have correctly filled in the Punnett Square, you can determine the phenotypes of the offspring. What are the phenotypes and genotypes of offspring in Situation 1?

_____

2. What are the phenotypes and genotypes of offspring in Situation 2? _____

_____

> **ALL IN THE FAMILY:** Examine your father, mother, brother, and sister for the following characteristics or traits that have been passed on from generation to generation. Don't forget to include yourself. Make a chart of your observations.
>
> Traits: right- or left-handed; dimples; attached or unattached ear lobes; cleft chin; light, dark, or red hair; freckles; connected or unconnected eyebrows; curly, wavy, or straight hair.

Commas. A *comma* is used to separate words or groups of words so that the meaning of a sentence is clear. Insert commas where they are needed in these sentences. If a sentence is correct, write C on the line.

1. I went to Sweden Norway and Denmark. _____

2. For lunch we had a tossed salad spaghetti and meatballs French bread Coke and fruit.

3. One of my favorite singers is Gloria Estefan who is the lead singer for the Miami Sound Machine._____

4. My ancestor Jonathan Livingston emigrated to America in the 1700s. _____

5. Who in your opinion deserves to get the English award this year? _____

6. However Lisa has been working hard lately and does all her work. _____

7. Are you going to the play tonight Dad? _____

8. Well I may not be the smartest kid in the class but I do try to do my best. ____

9. To prevent the teacher from calling her parents Beth decided to work._____

10. Over the hills and through the woods the little girl walked carefully. _____

Commas. There are probably more rules for commas than any other mark of punctuation. They are used in addresses and business letters. They are used after introductory words, phrases, and clauses. Read the following sentences, and insert commas where they are needed.

11. Because I had a headache last night my mom allowed me to do my homework early this morning.

12. The principal said he lived at 202 East Street Decatur Georgia.

13. Our Constitution was signed on September 17 1787 in Philadelphia Pennsylvania.

14. It was a long tiring climb to the top of the Washington Monument.

15. If I had to do it all over again I would certainly do the same thing.

16. Do you want to go and do you want me to get you a ticket?

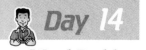

Word Problems
Solve the following problems using algebraic strategies when necessary.

1. Tom borrowed an amount of money from John. When he repaid John, he gave him $1,567.00. The arrangement was for Tom to repay the money, plus an additional $75.00. What was the original amount of money Tom borrowed?

2. In Mrs. Prince's art class, four-fifths of the class liked using the wheel to make clay items. Eight-twentieths of these students wanted to make a vase. What fraction of the class wanted to make clay items and a vase?

3. The Moores' delivery truck uses 40 gallons of gas each week making deliveries. It has been making deliveries for 10 weeks now. How much gas has it used?

4. Betsy has $45.00 in her savings account she planned to use for the family vacation. If she allowed herself to only spend $5.00 per day, how many days would this last?

5. Two groups of 24 students wanted to join the chorus. To make the whole group smaller, they divided it into 6 sections. How many students did each section have?

6. Only *y* students agreed to set up the sound equipment for the play. A total of *a* times *b* students said they would help with the lights. How many volunteers were there? (Give the expression.)

7. A group of girls went on an overnight camping trip. Six had to sleep in each tent. There were four tents. How many girls were on the trip?

8. Mr. Kemp wants to put a fence around his yard. His yard is square. The east side is 45 feet long. The south side is where the house is and needs no fencing. How much fencing material will he need?

9. Marsha went to buy a new car that cost $23,000.00, and the finance rate was 6%. She will pay interest over four years. How much interest will she pay in four years?

Political Parties.

1. What are the two main political parties in the United States?

2. What other parties have existed during American history?

New political parties (which are sometimes called "third parties") often form because a group wants things not strongly supported by one of the major two parties or because a group within a major party disagrees with the party in some way and breaks away from it. The ideas a party supports are called the party's "platform." Choose a "third party." What part or parts of its platform was (or is) it best known for?

Create a new political party. What would you name it? What would you use for a symbol? What would your platform be? What would make it different from the two main political parties?

Political Word Search.

Word Bank

democrat
republican
vote
citizen
rights
constitution
democracy
republic
bill of rights
responsibility
government
platform
political party
election

```
b y y b v z p b r k j j i p e
u t z g r o d b e r v y p n i
g r a j g f t p p e t c j c n
m a p t b j d e u s o a b o o
d p l l v n e y b p v r i n i
f l a d d e a p l o t c l s t
u a t e a z m r i n n o l t c
d c f m a i k o c s e m o i e
g i o o g t e s a i m e f t l
t t r c o i b t n b n d r u e
p i m r n c v h m i r t i t q
d l f a y y x g r l e d g i o
p o a t i h h i q i v n h o w
e p o p z o h r b t o g t n p
r e p u b l i c o y g u s n a
```

Mass and Inertia. The mass of an object is the amount of matter it contains. An object with mass has a quality called inertia. For example, if there is a ball resting on the ground, you have to push it to get it moving. You also have to give it another push to stop it again. If the ball is at rest, it wants to stay at rest; if the ball is moving, it wants to stay moving. This is called inertia.

Gravity and Weight. An object with mass attracts other objects with mass. This attraction is called gravity. Gravitational pull, or the attraction between two objects, is measured by weight. For example, when you get on a scale and weigh yourself, your weight is a measurement of the gravitational pull between you and the earth.

How Mass and Distance Effect Gravitational Pull. The strength of the gravitational force between two objects (measured by weight) depends on the their mass and how far apart they are. For example, if you were to double your mass, the gravitational pull between you and the earth would be twice as strong, and you would weigh more. If the planet you were standing on were twice as massive, the gravitational pull would also be twice as strong. On the other hand, the farther you get from the center of the planet, the weaker the gravitational force between you and the planet, and the less you would weigh.

Newton's Three Laws of Motion. Sir Isaac Newton discovered the force of gravity.

First Law: An object remains in motion or at rest unless acted on by a push or pull.
    A. As mass increases, inertia increases. As inertia increases, the amount of force needed to accelerate the object also increases.
    B. The opposite is also true. As an object's mass decreases, its inertia decreases, and the force needed to cause it to accelerate decreases.
    C. When an object accelerates, its velocity changes. To change velocity, a force must act on the object.

Second Law: The force on an object equals the mass of the object times the acceleration of the object. A force causes a mass to accelerate.
Force = Mass x Acceleration

Third Law: For every action there is an equal and opposite reaction. The action and reaction occur at exactly the same time.

Time Out:

1. You are an astronaut leaving on a mission to the moon. As you leave the earth and enter space, will you weigh less or more? _____

2. If you weigh 120 pounds on earth, what is your mass on the moon? _____

3. What does the word *inertia* mean? _____

4. Which rock would take more force to move, a 20-pound rock or a 40-pound rock?

Answer Pages

Page 3
1. interrogative   2. declarative   3. interrogative
4. interrogative   5. declarative   6. declarative
7. declarative   8. declarative   9. imperative

Page 4
1. 206.9   2. 54.926   3. 72.6936   4. 64.276
5. 854.41   6. 15.1   7. 39.1   8. 25.1
9. 26   10. 2   11. 96   12. 3 pictures
13. \$23.00   14. \$6.75   15. \$57.85   16. \$124.00

Page 5

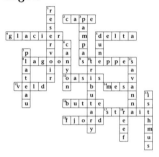

Page 6
1. crust   2. fracture   3. stress
4. fault   5. Tension   6. normal fault
7. lateral fault   8. plateau   9. hanging wall
10. F-magma   11. F-fault block mountains
12. F-crust   13. T   14. T

<u>TIME OUT</u>: Possible Answer: Plateaus can be formed when forces slowly push horizontally on an area, therefore causing an uplift. Plateaus can also be formed by a series of lava flows that spread, fill in areas and build up. Plateaus, unlike mountains, are flat-topped rather than peaked.

Page 7
1. run-on   2. fragment   3. sentence   4. fragment
5. run-on   6. run-on   7. prep. p.   8. part. p.
9. ger. p.   10. prep. p.   11. app. p.   12. app. p.
13. inf. p.   14. ger. p.   15. part. p.

Page 8
1. 18.82   2. 1.89   3. 16.99   4. 2,211.75
5. 166.42   6. 42,751.93 7. 21.22   8. 3.88
9. 7.81   10. 13.60 ÷ 15 = 91¢ per gallon
11. 42 x 12.4 = 520.8 inches tall
12. 23.5 ÷ 2 = 11.75 mph
13. 12.8 x 15 = 192 birdhouses

Page 9 • North America
1. Greenland, Nuuk (Godthåb)
2. Canada, Ottawa
3. United States, Washington, D.C.
4. Mexico, Mexico City
5. Guatemala, Guatemala City
6. Belize, Belmopan   7. Honduras, Tegucigalpa
8. El Salvador, San Salvador 9. Nicaragua, Managua
10. Costa Rica, San José   11. Panama, Panama City
12. Trinidad and Tobago, Port-of-Spain
13. Puerto Rico, San Juan   14. Hispaniola
15. Jamaica, Kingston   16. Cuba, Havana
17. Bahamas, Nassau   18. Gulf of Mexico

19. Atlantic Ocean   20. Hudson Bay
21. Arctic Ocean   22. Pacific Ocean
23. Colorado River   24. Mississippi River
25. Mackenzie River

Page 10

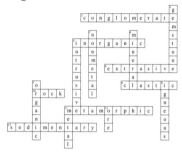

Page 11
1. time-d.o.   2. Jennifer-d.o.
3. sister-i.o.; cake-d.o.   4. none
5. ships-d.o.   6. merchants-i.o.; goods-d.o.
7. students, friends-d.o.   8. students-i.o.; guarantee-d.o.
9. none   10. puppy-i.o.; food-d.o.
11. great
12. These, snow-covered, visited, frequently-adv
13. spectacular, opening, Olympic
14. their, empty; Quickly-adv
15. burning, big, birthday, brightly, very-adv
16. seven; carefully, wisely-adv.
17. thick, dark, four, quietly-adv.
18. much, her, today, proudly-adv.
19. sick, hungry
20. proud, school, anxiously-adv.

Page 12
1. 8/49   2. 15/64   3. 8/27   4. 6/15   5. 2/15
6. 2/5   7. 7/15   8. 1/4   9. 5/18   10. 12/35
11. 5/16   12. 5/24   13. 28/45   14. 3/5   15. 14/99
16. 1/3 for flowers 17. 3/8 of a pound 18. 8/45 of the pages

Page 13 • Caribbean
1. Atlantic Ocean   2. Gulf of Mexico
3. Caribbean Sea   4. Greater Antilles
5. Lesser Antilles
6. Netherlands Antilles, Willemstad
7. Puerto Rico, San Juan
8. Dominican Republic, Santo Domingo
9. Cuba, Havana   10. Jamaica, Kingston
11. The Bahamas   11. b. Nassau
12. British Virgin Islands   13. U.S. Virgin Islands
14. Antigua & Barbuda, St. Johns
15. Guadeloupe, Basse-Terre
16. Saint Kitts and Nevis, Basseterre
17. Montserrat, Plymouth   18. Dominica, Roseau
19. Martinique, Fort-de-France
20. Saint Lucia, Castries
21. St. Vincent & the Grenadines, Kingstown
22. Barbados, Bridgetown   23. Grenada, St. George's
24. Tobago   25. Trinidad, Port-of-Spain
26. Bonaire   27. Curacao
28. Aruba, Oranjestad   29. Cayman Islands,
30. Straits of Florida   George Town
31. Turks & Caicos Islands, Grand Turk (Cockburn Town)
32. Haiti, Port-au-Prince

Page 15
1. dangerous-p.a. 2. swampy-p.a. 3. president-p.n.
4. car-p.n. 5. playwright-p.n. 6. captain-p.n.
7. book-p.n. 8. cool-p.a. 9. he-p.n.
10. impressive-p.a.

Page 16
1. 5 3/5 2. 7 2/5 3. 2 5/7
4. 6 5/6 5. 7 7/8 6. 55/99 & 27/99
7. 16/40 & 25/40
8. 49/91 & 65/91
9. 42/238 & 153/238
10. 1 9/77 11. 1 31/72 12. 5 13/14
13. 2 2/15 14. 1 53/126 15. 1/2
16. 2 43/56 17. 1 23/24 18. 2 17/35
19. 6 39/40 20. 21/40, yes

Page 17 • Northern Africa
1. Mediterranean Sea 2. Canary Islands
3. Morocco, Rabat 4. Algeria, Algiers
5. Tunisia, Tunis 6. Libya, Tripoli
7. Egypt, Cairo 8. Western Sahara, El Aaiún
9. Mauritania, Nouakchott 10. Mali, Bamako
11. Niger, Niamey 12. Chad, N'Djamena
13. Sudan, Khartoum 14. Eriteria, Asmara

Page 18
1. F 2. T 3. T 4. F 5. F
6. A 7. B 8. C 9. D 10. B

Page 19
1. since it began in the early 1600s
2. If it rains again today
3. that Mr. Barksdale told us to do
4. Even though our team tried hard to win the championship
5. that I lost yesterday on the bus
6. because she stayed up last night to study and review
7. If my father doesn't pick me up at school
8. which is the only white house on the block
9. While Randy cut and raked the grass

Page 20
1. 10 2/3 2. 12 1/2 3. 8 4. 28 5. 8
6. 16 7. 18 8. 9 9. 36 10. 3
11. 25 12. 14 2/9 13. 12 14. 10 7/17 15. 39 1/9
16. 8 rabbits, 10 fish, 2 dogs 17. $15.00 18. 11 rocks

Page 21 • Sub-Saharan Africa
1. Senegal, Dakar 2. The Gambia, Banjul
3. Guinea-Bissau, Bissau 4. Sierra Leone, Freetown
5. Guinea, Conakry 6. Liberia, Monrovia
7. Ivory Coast, Yamoussoukro
8. Burkina Faso, Ouagadougou
9. Ghana, Accra 10. Togo, Lomé
11. Benin, Porto-Novo 12. Nigeria, Abuja
13. Cameroon, Yaoundé
14. Central African Republic, Bangui
15. Equatorial Guinea, Malabo
16. Gabon, Libreville
17. Republic of Congo, Brazzaville
18. Cabinda, Cabinda 19. Angola, Luanda
20. Namibia, Windhoek
21. South Africa, Cape Town
22. Lesotho, Maseru 23. Swaziland, Mbabane
24. Botswana, Gaborone 25. Zimbabwe, Harare
26. Zambia, Lusaka 27. Mozambique, Maputo
28. Malawi, Lilongwe 29. Tanzania, Dodoma
30. Burundi, Bujumbura
31. Democratic Republic of the Congo, Kinshasa
32. Rwanda, Kigali 33. Lake Victoria
34. Uganda, Kampala 35. Kenya, Nairobi
36. Ethiopia, Addis Ababa 37. Somalia, Mogadishu
38. Djibouti, Djibouti 39. Madagascar, Antananarivo

Page 23
1. comes, s 2. were, p 3. create, p
4. is, s 5. are, p 6. was, s
7. walk, p 8. doesn't, s 9. shows, s
10. were, p 11. Everyone's 12. boys'
13. boy's 14. children's 15. girls'
16. cities' 17. puppy's 18. hour's
19. Mike's 20. car's

Page 24
1. 14/16 2. 2/3 3. 2/4 4. 10/70 5. 60/100
6. 3/18 7. 5/4 8. 24/56 9. 8/24 10. 1/12
11. No 12. Yes 13. No 14. Yes 15. No
16. No 17. Yes 18. No 19. < 20. <
21. > 22. > 23. > 24. = 25. >
26. = 27. = 28. = 29. Mark 30. Ann

Page 25 • Middle East
1. Azerbaijan, Baku 2. Armenia, Yerevan
3. Turkey, Ankara 4. Cyprus, Nicosia
5. Syria, Damascus 6. Lebanon, Beirut
7. Israel, Jerusalem 8. Jordan, Amman
9. Iraq, Baghdad 10. Iran, Tehran
11. Afghanistan, Kabul 12. Saudi Arabia, Riyadh
13. Kuwait, Kuwait City 14. Bahrain, Manama
15. Qatar, Doha
16. United Arab Emirates, Abu Dhabi
17. Oman, Muscat 18. Yemen, Sanaa

Page 26
1. troposphere, stratosphere, ionosphere, exosphere
2. meteorologist 3. Ben Franklin
4. red, orange, yellow, green, blue, indigo, violet
5. Condensed moisture is suspended in air.
6. rain 7. United States of America
8. moist subtropical
9. the percent of moisture the air holds relative to the amount it could hold at a particular temperature
10. canopy
11. temperature, precipitation, elevation
12. Answers will vary. 13. 23.5
14. around the equator

Page 28
1. 5 2/5 2. 5 11/56 3. 8 1/30
4. 4 2/5 5. 11 41/45 6. 5 7/20
7. 6 7/15 8. 9 3/10 9. 26 25/36
10. 3 11/29 11. 2 50/87 12. 4 13/32
13. 7 1/2 pies 14. 1/12 of the pages
15. 4 1/6 shares per niece

Answer Pages

Page 29 • Northern Asia
1. Russia, Moscow
2. Estonia, Tallinn
3. Latvia, Riga
4. Lithuania, Vilnius
5. Belarus, Minsk
6. Ukraine, Kiev
7. Turkey, Ankara
8. Armenia, Yerevan
9. Azerbaijan, Baku
10. Georgia, Tbilisi
11. Turkmenistan, Ashgabat
12. Uzbekistan, Tashkent
13. Kazakhstan, Astana
14. Afghanistan, Kabul
15. Tajikistan, Dushanbe
16. Kyrgyzstan, Bishkek

Page 30
1. A 　　2. C 　　3. D 　　4. B 　　5. B
6. B 　　7. A 　　8. D 　　9. B

Page 31
1. X don't
2. X best; add better
3. X no; add any
4. X more
5. X good; add well
6. X tallest; add taller
7. X more; add best
8. X -n't
9. X most
10. X gooder; add better
11. X -est; add most
12. X more
13. on-prep
14. Wait-int; on-prep
15. and-conj; by-prep
16. In-prep
17. to-prep; but-conj; in-prep
18. for-prep; and-conj
19. and-conj; to-prep
20. Wow-int

Page 32
1. 5.425 　　2. 3.8316 　　3. .7569 　　4. 851.0121
5. 3.538 　　6. 268.145 　　7. 7.2599 　　8. 25.556
9. 5.4832 　　10. 2.244 　　11. 38.967 　　12. 21.3123
13. 28.432 　　14. 6.9332 　　15. 16.666 　　16. 417.81
17. 11.189 　　18. 675.492 　　19. 5.154 　　20. 3.116 miles
21. 2.55 yards 　　22. 8.38 gallons

Page 35 • Asia/Southeast Asia
1. Japan, Tokyo
2. South Korea, Seoul
3. North Korea, Pyongyang
4. Mongolia, Ulaanbaatar
5. Pakistan, Islamabad
6. India, New Delhi
7. China, Beijing
8. Nepal, Kathmandu
9. Bhutan, Thimphu
10. Bangladesh, Dhaka
11. Myanmar (Burma), Rangoon (Yangon)
12. Laos, Vientiane
13. Thailand, Bangkok
14. Cambodia, Phnom Penh 15. Vietnam, Hanoi
16. Malaysia, Kuala Lumpur
17. Singapore, Singapore City
18. Brunei, Bandar Seri Begawan
19. Indonesia, Jakarta
20. Philippines, Manila
21. Taiwan, Taipei

Page 37
1. C 　　2. C 　　3. A 　　4. B
5. A 　　6. B 　　7. C 　　8. B

9.

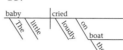

10.

11.

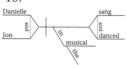

12.

13.

14.

15.

Page 38
1. .33 　　2. .17 　　3. .875 　　4. .6
5. .625 　　6. .67 　　7. .78 　　8. .5
9. 8/10 or 4/5 　　10. 78/100 or 39/50
11. 9/10 　　12. 57/100
13. 6/100 or 3/50 　　14. 12/100 or 3/25
15. 26/100 or 13/50 　　16. 43/100
17. 2 　　18. 72/100 or 18/25
19. 8 　　20. 4
21. 1 25/100 or 1 1/4 　　22. 3/100
23. 22 　　24. 429
25. 88/1000 or 11/125

Page 39 • Oceania
1. Papua New Guinea, Port Moresby
2. Northern Territory, Darwin
3. Western Australia, Perth
4. South Australia, Adelaide
5. Queensland, Brisbane
6. New South Wales, Sydney
7. Capital Territory, Canberra
8. Victoria, Melbourne
9. Tasmania, Hobart
10. New Zealand, Wellington
11. South Island
12. North Island
13. New Caledonia, Nouméa
14. Fiji, Suva
15. Vanuatu, Port-Vila
16. Solomon Islands, Honiara

Page 40
1. motor vehicles
2. diesel motors
3. about 8.4%
4. industries
5. Examples—carpooling, walking, bicycling, using public transportation, more effective and better emission control system

Page 41
1. fish, fries,
2. Copenhagen,
3. Seattle,
4. party,
5. Street, Decatur,
6. Heather,
7. lonely, road,
8. Donna, 2,
9. Sanders, M.D., Atlanta,

10.

11.

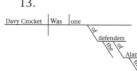

12.

13.

Answer Pages

Page 42
1. 3%   2. 12%   3. 25%   4. 84%
5. .17   6. 39%   7. 77/100   8. .35
9. 47%   10. 36/100 11. 204%   12. 1 38/100
13. 7.65   14. 12%

Page 43 • Europe
A. Barents Sea   B. Norwegian Sea   C. Atlantic Sea
D. North Sea   E. Baltic Sea   F. Black Sea
G. Mediterranean Sea
1. Malta, Valletta   2. Italy, Rome
3. San Marino, San Marino   4. Vatican City
5. France, Paris   6. Monaco, Monaco
7. Spain, Madrid
8. Andorra, Andorra La Vella
9. Portugal, Lisbon   10. Switzerland, Bern
11. Austria, Vienna   12. Liechtenstein, Vaduz
13. Kaliningrad, Kaliningrad 14. Belgium, Brussels
15. Netherlands, Amsterdam 16. Germany, Berlin
17. Denmark, Copenhagen   18. Iceland, Reykjavik
19. Finland, Helsinki   20. Sweden, Stockholm
21. Norway, Oslo   22. Greece, Athens
23. Ireland, Dublin   24. England, London
25. Wales, Cardiff   26. Scotland, Edinburgh
27. N. Ireland, Belfast
28. Gibraltar
29. Russia, Moscow   30. Poland, Warsaw
31. Ukraine, Kiev   32. Belarus, Minsk
33. Romania, Bucharest   34. Hungary, Budapest
35. Lithuania, Vilnius   36. Latvia, Riga
37. Estonia, Tallinn   38. Bulgaria, Sofia
39. Albania, Tirana   40. Czech Republic, Prague
41. Slovak Republic, Bratislava
42. Bosnia-Herzegovina, Sarajevo
43. Croatia, Zagreb   44. Slovenia, Ljubljana
45. Moldova, Chisinău   46. Macedonia, Skopje
47. Serbia, Belgrade   48. Turkey, Ankara

Page 44
1. T   2. F   3. T   4. F   5. T
6. D   7. B   8. C   9. A   10. B

Page 45
1. Daniel's house   2. He ran.   3. new car
4. black   5. A car was following him.
6. Responses will vary.

Page 46
1. 144   2. 22.4   3. 15
4. 760.5   5. 10.08   6. 153.7
7. 44.55   8. 72   9. $126.00
10. 42%   11. $36,645.00 12. $240.00

Page 47
1. Cairo, Egypt   2. Wellington, New Zealand
3. Capetown, South Africa 4. Berlin, Germany
5. San Diego, California 6. Chicago, Illinois
7. Hong Kong, China   8. Paris, France
9. Beijing, China   10. Buenos Aires, Argentina
11. Toronto, Canada   12. Caracas, Venezuela
13. 22°S 43°W   14. 51°N 0°
15. 19°N 73°E   16. 26°S 28°E
17. 36°N 140°E   18. 19°N 99°W
19. 42°N 12°E   20. 55°N 37°E
21. 34°N 118°W   22. 41°N 73°W
23. 35°S 149°E   24. 46°N 77°W

Page 48
1. D—not a fossil fuel
2. A—not public transportation
3. D—cannot be used again
4. C—not a natural resource
5. C—not one of the three major types of pollution
6. C   7. D   8. A   9. E   10. B

Page 49
1. Walden, "Economy"
2. baby-sitter, The Little Mermaid
3. "Leave...home," "Your...trip."
4. mid-July,
5. Curtis—...mean—
6. "At...morning," "someone...dollars."
7. Tennessee, e's, n's, s's
8. Scandinavian Queen   9. America;
10. items: 11. 7: 8:
12. Hungary; Australia;   13. class;
14. act;   15. 1: 3:

Page 50
1. $31,200.00   2. $448,800.00   3. $90.00
Chart Answers:
1. $66.40   2. $5.12   3. $360.00
4. $108.00   5. $59.36   6. $3.12
7. $58.50   8. $600.00   9. $792.00
10. $60,000.00 11. $2,430,000.00 12. $7,875.00
13. $57,600.00 14. $9,800,000.00

Page 51
1. around major rivers; bodies of water
2. Mekong, Red, Irrawaddy, Chow Phrayo
3. Indonesia
4. New Guinea and Borneo, Sabah and Sarawak
5. Java
6. Philippines
7. Laos and Cambodia
8. population clusters or distribution of population; one dot equals 100,000 people

Page 52
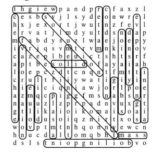

Page 53
1. B   2. C   3. A   4. D

Answer Pages

Page 54

1. line
2. line segment
3. ray
4. angle
5. acute
6. right
7. obtuse
8. acute

9.
10.
11.

Page 55

1. For every American dollar you would receive about 1.75 or 1 3/4 Australian dollars.
2. B. 3,555 pesos, 1,855 pesos, $2.40; C. 32.15 yuan; $1.14; D. $1.97; $3.03; E. 23.45 shekels; $2.70

Page 56

1. Mixture—matter that consists of 2 or more substances mixed, but not chemically combined. Solution—homogeneous mixture in which one substance is dissolved in another. Element—simplest type of pure substance.
2. Heterogeneous Mixture—substance that does not appear to be the same throughout. Homogeneous Mixture—substance that appears to be the same throughout.
3. insoluble
4. List varies: N, P, As, Bi, O, S, Al, Pb, Sn, C, Li, Na, K, Mg, Ca, Ba, Ra, U, Co, Ni, Cu, Zn, F, Cl, He, Ne, Ar, Kr, As, Fe, Br, I, Rn, Xe.
5. Compound—substance made up of molecules that contain more than one kind of atom; two or more elements chemically combined.
6. Atom—smallest particle of an element that has all the properties of that element. Molecule—structure made up of two or more atoms.
7. $2H_2 + O_2 = 2H_2O$
8. (1) All elements are composed of atoms. Atoms are individual and indestructible particles. (2) Atoms of the same element are exactly alike. (3) Atoms of different elements are different. (4) Compounds are formed by the joining together of atoms of two or more elements.
9. proton, neutron, electron   10. proton, neutron
11. number of protons in the nucleus of an atom
12. number of protons and neutrons in an atom's nucleus
13. circling outside the nucleus
14. 79 protons are in the atom's nucleus.

Page 57

1. main topics
2. yes
3. A. Underwater robot   B. New information
4. page number
5. author's last name
6. author of article
7. page numbers of article
8. "Down into the Deep"

Page 58

1. perimeter = 16 in.
2. area = 15 in.²
3. perimeter = 28 in.
4. area = 48 in.²
5. perimeter = 20 cm
6. area = 21 cm²
7. perimeter = 24 mm
8. area = 24 mm²
9. perimeter = 28 cm
10. area = 43 cm²
11. perimeter = 18 cm
12. area = 20 cm²
13. perimeter = 28 in.
14. area = 28 in.²
15. perimeter = 16 in.
16. area = 12 in.²

Page 59

1. Tenochtitlan
2. Statue of Liberty
3. Panama
4. Machu Picchu
5. CN Tower
6. Chichen Itza
7. Brasilia
8. Vatican City
9. Stonehenge
10. Parthenon
11. Kremlin
12. Angkor Wat
13. Great Wall of China
14. Sydney Opera House
15. Taj Mahal
16. Great Pyramid at Giza

Page 60

[crossword puzzle with answers: chlorine, silver, neon, nickel, oxygen, radon, uranium, sodium]

Page 61

1. D   2. C   3. A   4. D
5. D   6. C   7. D   8. C

Page 62

1. 3   2. 14   3. 10   4. -30   5. 2   6. -89
7. 56   8. 165   9. -1   10. 14   11. -2   12. -22
13. 5   14. -5   15. -24   16. -9   17. 24   18. 4
19. 14   20. -4   21. -9   22. 1   23. 5   24. 7
25. -10   26. 4   27. 4   28. 13   29. -4

Page 63

1. Pakistan   2. Pakistan   3. Buddhism   4. India
5. Sri Lanka   6. Nepal   7. Nepal   8. Sri Lanka
9. Bangladesh, Pakistan

Page 65

1. B   2. C   3. D   4. A   5. C   6. B
7. D   8. B   9. A   10. C   11. D   12. B
13. C   14. A   15. A   16. B

Page 66

1. -72   2. -30   3. -28   4. -8   5. -36   6. -49
7. 70   8. -72   9. -24   10. -25   11. -12   12. -22
13. -20   14. 24   15. -108   16. -30   17. -7   18. -9
19. -7   20. -7   21. 7   22. -5   23. -4   24. -12
25. -9   26. floor 8   27. floor 1

Answer Pages

Page 68
1. 13   2. 26   3. aluminum 4. D
5. B   6. C   7. A   8. D
9. B   10. D

Page 69
1. B   2. D   3. A   4. C   5. B
6. D   7. A   8. D   9. toward 10. within
11. beneath 12. again 13. kill 14. self 15. small
16. foot 17. three 18. earth 19. sound 20. say

Page 70
1. 5   2. 4   3. 7   4. 11   5. 41   6. 36
7. 25   8. 9   9. 16   10. 10   11. 18   12. 12
13. 2^5 14. 5^4 15. 7^6 16. 8^3 17. 10^4 18. 3^5
19. <   20. >   21. =   22. <   23. <   24. <

Page 72
1. cochlea   2. semicircular canals
3. stirrup   4. anvil
5. hammer   6. auricle
7. external auditory canal   8. bones
9. eardrum   10. eustachian tube
11. cochlear nerve   12. vestibular nerve
1. T   2. T   3. F   4. T   5. F
6. T   7. T   8. T   9. F   10. T

Page 73
1. draw   2. fear of   3. good   4. with
5. cut   6. two   7. faith   8. write
9. A   10. B   11. C

Page 74
1. $43.00   2. $3.83   3. .8 kg
4. 1 liter   5. 33/40   6. 96
7. 17.6 meters   8. $210.00   9. $350.00
10. $1,300.00

Page 78
1. C   2. D   3. B   4. A   5. C   6. D

Page 79

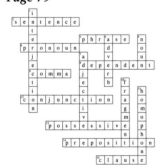

Page 80
1. 12   2. 14   3. 60   4. 30
5. 85   6. 6   7. 10   8. 78
9. 106   10. 280   11. 7   12. 39
13. 81   14. n − 7   15. 2 + 3n   16. 9n − 8
17. n − 5   18. n + 4   19. 5n + 6n   20. n ÷ 12

Page 82
1. iris   2. lens   3. pupil
4. cornea   5. vitreous humor
6. retina   7. optic nerve
1. T   2. T   3. T   4. F   5. F   6. T
7. F   8. F   9. T   10. T   11. photon
12. ultraviolet   13. light 14. book 15. incandescent

Page 83
1. drifted—intr   2. drove—tr; repaired—tr
3. wrote—intr   4. wrote—tr
5. was delivered—intr   6. hiked—tr
7. is—This…building   8. looks—car…good
9. would have tasted—anything…delicious
10. was—kitten…small   11. felt—he…embarrassed
12. is—Zac…president   13. is—He…Sam
14. looked—Seth…tired, happy
15 none   16. looked—train…upset
17. is—This…she   18. none

Page 84
1. -3 2/3   2. -2   3. c=2   4. q=3/2   5. -6
6. 41   7. 74   8. 7   9. -10   10. -19
11. =   12. <   13. =   14. <   15. >   16. >

Page 86

Page 87
1. Toni, Italy,   2. C   3. C
4. Chicago,   5. Vanessa, athlete, 6. *Giver,*
7. correspondent, McCoy,   8. her
9. his   10. his or her   11. they
12. herself   13. his or her   14. he, his
15. he or she   16. themselves   17. one's

Page 88
1. 29ab   2. -8y   3. 5x + ax   4. 10x + 5ay
5. 18a   6. b + 3c + 2   7. -8cd   8. -8x + 4
9. 2xy − 3b   10. a + 1   11. 10x − 5   12. 5x + 3y + p
13. 3a − 2b + 3c   14. 7x − y + 32
15. -ax + 3bx + 4x   16. 7x − 3a − 4b
17. 5n − 8a − 2b   18. 3x − 9y
19. -2bx + 4x   20. 10n + 1

Page 90
1. mouth   2. teeth   3. salivary glands
4. esophagus   5. stomach   6. liver
7. gall bladder   8. pancreas   9. small intestine
10. large intestine 11. rectum
1. may help in immunity   2. 12–24 hours
3. liver   4. pancreas
5. molars, premolars, canines, incisors   6. epiglottis

Answer Pages

Page 91
1. A 2. C 3. A 4. D
5. C 6. desert 7. hear 8. led
9. peace 10. stationery 11. There
12. quite 13. too, to, to

Page 92
1. x = 4.67 2. x = 3.75 3. x = 2 4. x = 9
5. x = 2 6. x = 4 7. x = 5 8. x = 3
9. x = 10 10. x = 1 11. x = -.5 12. -15 = b
13. -3 = p 14. -20 = a 15. -5 = a 16. -4 = m
17. x = 0 18. x = 0

Page 94
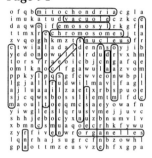

Page 95
1. F 2. F 3. S 4. S
5. F 6. S 7. S 8. F
9. S 10. F 11. , and it 12. . Also
13. C 14. . It 15. , and they 16. C
17. , and everyone

Page 96
1. 10ax + 3a 2. -9x – 7y 3. 9ab – 18q
4. 5x – 9 5. 11y – 16z 6. 5x + 5
7. -ab – c 8. 4ay + 7y 9. -9a – 9b
10. 2b + 1 11. 0 12. 13y + 5z
13. -9b + 3c 14. 7ab – 3c 15. 2y – 4b

Page 98
1. Carbon dioxide gas from the atmosphere enters the leaf through openings called stomata.
2. Plants can make their own food by using the energy of sunlight and inorganic chemicals.
3. The oxygen gas is released into the atmosphere. It is then used by animals.
4. The energy comes from photons of light striking a green chemical called chlorophyll. Electrons in chlorophyll are energized and are used to split H_2O.

Page 99
1. X-most 2. X- worser; worse
3. X- most; more 4. add other after any
5. X- beautifulest; most beautiful
6. X- more 7. C
8. X- more 9. C
10. X- hasn't; has; or X- never; ever
11. X- no; any 12. X- no; any
13. X couldn't; could 14. X- no; any
15. X- no one; anyone 16. X- never; ever
17. X- nothing; anything 18. C

Page 100
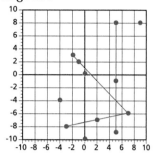

Page 102
Situation 1: Ww Ww Ww Ww
Situation 2: WW Ww Ww ww
1. phenotype: black; genotypes: Ww, Ww, Ww, Ww
2. phenotype: 3 black & 1 white; genotypes: WW, Ww, Ww, ww

Page 103
1. Sweden, Norway, 2. salad, meatballs, bread, Coke,
3. Estefan, 4. ancestor, Livingston,
5. Who, opinion, 6. However, 7. tonight,
8. Well, class, 9. parents, 10. woods,
11. night, 12. Street, Decatur, 13. 17, Philadelphia,
14. long, 15. again, 16. go,

Page 104
1. $1,492.00 2. 8/25 3. 400 gallons
4. 9 days 5. 8 students per section
6. y + ab 7. 24 girls
8. 135 feet 9. $5,520.00

Page 105
1. Democratic, Republican
2. Whig, Federalist, Populist, Socialist, Progressive, Green, American, Reform, Libertarian, etc.

Page 106
1. less
2. Your *mass* would remain the same.
3. Inertia is the tendency of matter to remain at rest (or to keep moving in the same direction) unless affected by some outside force.
4. It would take more force to move a 40-pound rock because it has more mass.

Using Latitude and Longitude. Use the map below to answer the questions and plot the locations on page 47.

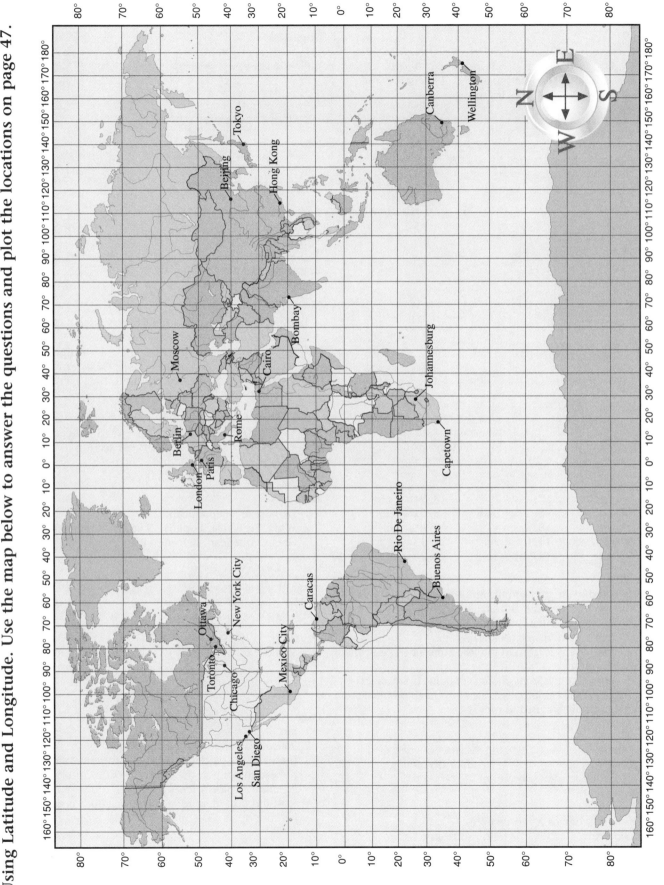

Page 47 Reference

Numbers

Natural—numbers used for counting (1, 2, 3, 4).
Composite—any number greater than one that has more than two factors.
Prime—any number greater than one that can only be factored by itself and the number one.
Whole—the set of natural numbers, plus zero.
Integers—any positive or negative whole number, plus zero.
Real—comprises all rational and irrational numbers, both positive and negative.

Number Line

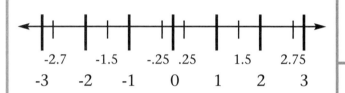

Negative   Origin   Positive

Special Lines

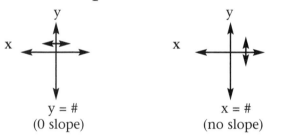

Integers Rules

1. When **adding** two numbers with the same sign, take the sum of the two numbers and keep the sign.
   Examples: 3 + 6 = 9; -2 + -4 = -6.
2. When **adding** two numbers with different signs, take the difference of the two numbers and use the sign of the larger number.
   Examples: -16 + 8 = -8; 7 + -3 = 4.
3. When **subtracting** two numbers, change the subtraction problem to an addition problem by adding the opposite of what was being subtracted. Follow steps #1 and #2 to finish the problem: Examples: -12 – 6 = -12 + -6 = 18;
   8 – -3 = 8 + 3 = 11

Rational Numbers

- When you add, subtract, or multiply 2 integers, the answer is an integer.
- The quotient of 2 integers is not always an integer.
- A **rational** number is any number that can be written as the quotient of 2 integers.
- **Irrational** numbers cannot be written as the quotient of 2 numbers.
- Whole numbers and their opposites are called integers.

Pythagorean Theorem

In a right angle triangle, the longest side is the hypotenuse; the other sides are the legs. The sum of the squares of the legs is equal to the square of the hypotenuse ($a^2 + b^2 = c^2$).

Order of Operations

1. Do work inside parentheses first.
2. Do any operations above or below a division bar.
3. Do all multiplication and division from left to right.
4. Do all addition and subtraction from left to right.

Formulas

Distance = Rate • Time
Income = Salary + Commission
Profit = Income – Expenses

Wet asphalt skid length = $\dfrac{\text{speed of car}^2}{160}$

Salary or wage =
    Hours worked • Pay/hourly rate = Money earned
Work done = Rate of work • Time
Total cost = Pounds • Price per pound
Interest = Principal • Interest rate • Time
Volume of a rectangular prism =
    length x width x height
Volume of a cylinder = area of base x height
Surface area of a rectangular prism = Find the area of each face and add the areas of all faces.
Surface area of cylinder =
    Add areas of 2 bases and area of the curved surface.

Area of a circle base = $\pi • r^2$
Area of a curved surface = $\pi • 2 • r • h$

QUICK REFERENCE CHART

CAPITALIZATION AND PUNCTUATION GUIDE

Capitalize:

- the first word of every sentence
- proper nouns and proper adjectives
- the first word in a direct quotation
- the first word in the greeting and the closing of a letter
- names of people and also the initials or abbreviations that stand for those names
- titles used with names of persons and abbreviations standing for those titles
- the first letter of the first, last, and other important words in a title
- names of the days of the week, months of the year, and special holidays
- names of languages, races, nationalities, religions, and proper adjectives formed from them
- the first word and all important words in titles of books, periodicals, poems, stories, articles, movies, paintings, and other works of art
- geographic names and sections of the country or world
- names of special events, historical events, government bodies, documents, and periods of time
- names of organizations, institutions, associations, teams, and their members
- names of businesses and brand names of their products
- abbreviations of titles and organizations
- words that refer to a specific deity and sacred books
- words denoting family relationships such as *mother, father, brother, aunt, uncle,* etc., only when these words stand for the name of the same individual

Punctuation Rules:

A period is used . . .
- at the end of a declarative sentence as well as a mild imperative sentence
- after initials and abbreviations
- after numbers and letters in outlines
- only once for a sentence ending with an abbreviation
- as a decimal point and to separate dollars and cents

A comma is used ...

- to separate words, phrases, or clauses in a series (at least three items)
- to set off a direct quotation
- to separate the names of a city and state in an address
- to separate the month and day from the year in a date
- to set off a word, phrase, or clause that interrupts the main thought of a sentence
- to separate a noun of direct address from the rest of the sentence
- to separate two or more adjectives which modify the same noun
- to enclose a title, name, or initials which follow a person's last name
- to separate an appositive or any other explanatory phrase from the rest of the sentence
- to separate two independent clauses in a compound sentence joined by such words as: *but, or, for, so, yet*
- to separate digits in a number to set off places of hundreds, thousands, millions
- to make the meaning clear whenever necessary

A semicolon is used ...

- to separate two independent clauses very close in meaning but not joined by *and, but, or, nor, for,* or *yet*
- to separate groups of words or phrases which already contain commas
- to connect two independent clauses when the second clause begins with a conjunctive adverb

A colon is used ...

- after the greeting of a formal letter
- before a list of items or details, especially after expressions such as *as follows* and *the following*
- before a long, formal statement or quotation
- between independent clauses when the second clause explains the first clause
- between the parts of a number which indicate time

Parentheses are used ...

- to enclose incidental explanatory matter which is added to a sentence but is not considered of major importance
- to enclose a question mark after a date or statement to show some doubt
- to enclose an author's insertion or comment

Dashes are used ...

- to indicate an abrupt break in thought in the sentence
- to mean *namely, in other words, that is,* etc. before an explanation

A hyphen is used ...

- to divide a word at the end of a line (divide only between syllables)
- to join the words in compound numbers from twenty-one to ninety-nine and with fractions used as adjectives
- with the prefixes *ex-, self-, all-,* with the suffix *-elect,* and with all prefixes before a proper noun or proper adjective
- to prevent confusion or awkwardness

A question mark is used ...

- at the end of a direct question (an interrogative sentence)
- inside quotation marks when the quotation is a question

An exclamation mark is used ...

- after a word, phrase, or sentence that expresses strong feeling
- inside quotation marks when the quotation is an exclamation

Quotation marks are used ...

- to set off a direct quotation—a person's exact words (Single quotation marks are used for quotes within quotes.)
- to enclose titles of articles, short stories, poems, songs and other parts of books and periodicals

Underlining (italics) is used ...

- for titles of books, plays, magazines, newspapers, films, ships, radio and TV programs, music albums, works of art
- to emphasize words, letters, and figures referred to as such and for foreign words

QUICK REFERENCE CHART

NORTH AMERICA

Country	Capital
Antigua & Barbuda	St. John's
Aruba	Oranjestad
Bahamas	Nassau
Barbados	Bridgetown
Bermuda	Hamilton
British Virgin Islands	Road Town
Canada	Ottawa
Cayman Islands	George Town
Cuba	Havana
Dominica	Roseau
Dominican Republic	Santo Domingo
Greenland	Godthaab
Grenada	St. George's
Guadeloupe	Basse-Terre
Haiti	Port-au-Prince
Jamaica	Kingston
Martinique	Fort-de-France
Montserrat	Plymouth
Netherlands Antilles	Willemstad
Puerto Rico	San Juan
Saint Kitts & Nevis	Basseterre
Saint Lucia	Castries
St. Pierre & Miquelon	St. Pierre
St. Vincent & Grenadines	Kingstown
Trinidad & Tobago	Port-of-Spain
Turks & Caicos Islands	Grand Turk
United States	Washington, D.C.
Virgin Islands of U.S.	Charlotte Amalie

CANADA

Province	Capital
Alberta	Edmonton
British Columbia	Victoria
Manitoba	Winnipeg
New Brunswick	Fredericton
Newfoundland and Labrador	St. John's
Nova Scotia	Halifax
Ontario	Toronto
Prince Edward Island	Charlottetown
Quebec	Quebec
Saskatchewan	Regina

Territory	Capital
Northwest Territories	Yellowknife
Yukon Territories	Whitehorse

CENTRAL AMERICA

Country	Capital
Belize	Belmopan
Costa Rica	San Jose
El Salvador	San Salvador
Guatemala	Guatemala City
Honduras	Tegucigalpa
Mexico	Mexico City
Nicaragua	Managua
Panama	Panama City

SOUTH AMERICA

Country	Capital
Argentina	Buenos Aires
Bolivia	La Paz/Sucre
Brazil	Brasilia
Chile	Santiago
Colombia	Bogota
Ecuador	Quito
Falkland Island	Stanley
French Guiana	Cayenne
Guyana	Georgetown
Paraguay	Asuncion
Peru	Lima
Suriname	Paramaribo
Uruguay	Montevideo
Venezuela	Caracas

QUICK REFERENCE CHART

EUROPE

Country	Capital
Albania	Tirane
Andorra	Andorra la Vella
Armenia	Yerevan
Austria	Vienna
Azerbaijan	Baku
Belarus	Minsk
Belgium	Brussels
Bosnia-Herzegovina	Sarajevo
Bulgaria	Sofia
Croatia	Zagreb
Czech Republic	Prague
Denmark	Copenhagen
Estonia	Tallinn
Finland	Helsinki
France	Paris
Georgia	Tbilisi
Germany	Berlin
Gibraltar	Gibraltar
Greece	Athens
Hungary	Budapest
Iceland	Reykjavik
Ireland	Dublin
Italy	Rome
Latvia	Riga
Liechtenstein	Vaduz
Lithuania	Vilnius
Luxembourg	Luxembourg
Macedonia	Skopje
Malta	Valletta
Moldova	Kishinev
Monaco	Monaco
Netherlands, The	Amsterdam
Norway	Oslo
Poland	Warsaw
Portugal	Lisbon
Romania	Bucharest
Russia	Moscow
San Marino	San Marino
Slovakia	Bratislava
Slovenia	Ljubljana
Spain	Madrid
Sweden	Stockholm
Switzerland	Bern
Ukraine	Kiev
United Kingdom	London
Vatican City	Vatican City
Yugoslavia	Belgrade

UNITED STATES

State	Capital
Alabama	Montgomery
Alaska	Juneau
Arizona	Phoenix
Arkansas	Little Rock
California	Sacramento
Colorado	Denver
Connecticut	Hartford
Delaware	Dover
Florida	Tallahassee
Georgia	Atlanta
Hawaii	Honolulu
Idaho	Boise
Illinois	Springfield
Indiana	Indianapolis
Iowa	Des Moines
Kansas	Topeka
Kentucky	Frankfort
Louisiana	Baton Rouge
Maine	Augusta
Maryland	Annapolis
Massachusetts	Boston
Michigan	Lansing
Minnesota	St. Paul
Mississippi	Jackson
Missouri	Jefferson City
Montana	Helena
Nebraska	Lincoln
Nevada	Carson City
New Hampshire	Concord
New Jersey	Trenton
New Mexico	Santa Fe
New York	Albany
North Carolina	Raleigh
North Dakota	Bismarck
Ohio	Columbus
Oklahoma	Oklahoma City
Oregon	Salem
Pennsylvania	Harrisburg
Rhode Island	Providence
South Carolina	Columbia
South Dakota	Pierre
Tennessee	Nashville
Texas	Austin
Utah	Salt Lake City
Vermont	Montpelier
Virginia	Richmond
Washington	Olympia
West Virginia	Charleston
Wisconsin	Madison
Wyoming	Cheyenne

QUICK REFERENCE CHART
Periodic Table

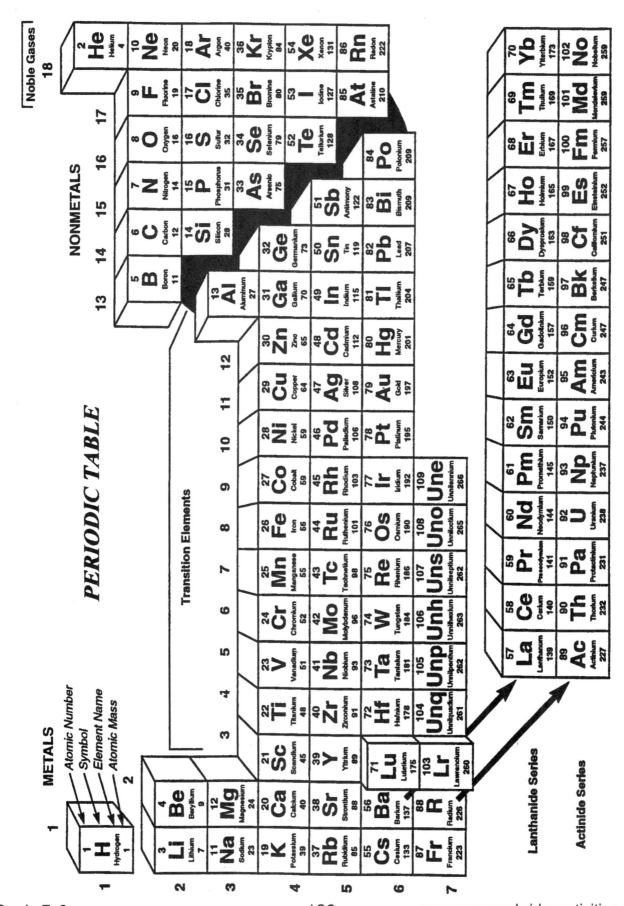

Notes

5 Five things I'm thankful for:

1. _____
2. _____
3. _____
4. _____
5. _____

Notes

5 Five things I'm thankful for:

1. _____
2. _____
3. _____
4. _____
5. _____

Notes

5 Five things I'm thankful for:

1. _____
2. _____
3. _____
4. _____
5. _____

Notes

Five things I'm thankful for:

1. _____
2. _____
3. _____
4. _____
5. _____

Notes

Five things I'm thankful for:

1. _____
2. _____
3. _____
4. _____
5. _____

Notes

5 Five things I'm
thankful for:

1. _____
2. _____
3. _____
4. _____
5. _____

Up until now, Summer Bridge Activities has been all about your mind…

But the other parts of you—who you are, how you act, and how you feel—are important too. That's why this year we are introducing a whole new section in Summer Bridge Activities: Building Better Bodies and Behavior. These new pages are all about helping build a better you this summer.

Keeping your body strong and healthy helps you live better, learn better, and feel better. To keep your body healthy, you need to do things like eat right, get enough sleep, and exercise. The Physical Fitness pages of Building Better Bodies will teach you about good eating habits and the importance of proper exercise. You can even train for a Presidential Fitness Award over the summer.

The Character pages are all about building a better you on the inside. They've got fun activities for you and your family to do together. The activities will help you develop important values and habits you'll need as you grow up.

After a summer of Building Better Bodies and Behavior and Summer Bridge Activities, there may be a whole new you ready for school in the fall!

For Parents: Introduction to Character Education

Character education is simply giving your child clear messages about the values you and your family consider important. Many studies have shown that a basic core of values is universal. You will find certain values reflected in the laws of every country and incorporated in the teachings of religious, ethical, and other belief systems throughout the world.

The character activities included here are designed to span the entire summer. Each week your child will be introduced to a new value, with a quote and two activities that illustrate it. Research has shown that character education is most effective when parents reinforce the values in their child's daily routine; therefore, we encourage parents to be involved as their child completes the lessons.

Here are some suggestions on how to maximize these lessons.
- Read through the lesson yourself. Then set aside a block of time when you and your child discuss the value.
- Plan a block of time to work on the suggested activities.
- Discuss the meaning of the quote with your child. Ask, "What do you think the quote means?" Have your child ask other members of the family the same question. If possible, include grandparents, aunts, uncles, and cousins.
- Use the quote as often as you can during the week. You'll be pleasantly surprised to learn that both you and your child will have it memorized.
- For extra motivation, you can set a reward for completing each week's activities.
- Point out to your child other people who are actively displaying a value. Example: "See how John is helping Mrs. Olsen by raking her leaves."
- Be sure to praise your child each time he or she practices a value: "Mary, it was very courteous of you to wait until I finished speaking."
- Find time in your day to talk about values. Turn off the radio in the car and chat with your children; take a walk in the evening as a family; read a story about the weekly value at bedtime; or give a back rub while you talk about what makes your child happy or sad.
- Finally, model the values you want your child to acquire. Remember, children will do as you do, not as you say.

Name _____ Date _____

How I Measure Up!

You will be filling out this page twice—once now and once at the end of the summer to see how you have grown. Have someone help you measure yourself to fill in the blanks below. Write your answers in inches.

smile ___ / ___

around the neck ___ / ___

neck to belly button ___ / ___

around the wrist ___ / ___

waist to ankle ___ / ___

foot length ___ / ___

shoulder to elbow ___ / ___

elbow to wrist ___ / ___

around the waist ___ / ___

length of longest finger ___ / ___

around the knee ___ / ___

around the ankle ___ / ___

length of longest finger ___ / ___

around the wrist ___ / ___

neck to belly button ___ / ___

around the waist ___ / ___

waist to ankle ___ / ___

foot length ___ / ___

smile ___ / ___

around the neck ___ / ___

shoulder to elbow ___ / ___

elbow to wrist ___ / ___

around the knee ___ / ___

around the ankle ___ / ___

Nutrition

The food you eat helps your body grow and gives you energy to work and play. Some foods give you protein or fats. Other foods provide vitamins, minerals, or carbohydrates. These are all things your body needs. Eating lots of different foods from the five major food groups every day can help you stay healthy.

Each day your body needs several servings of food from each group:

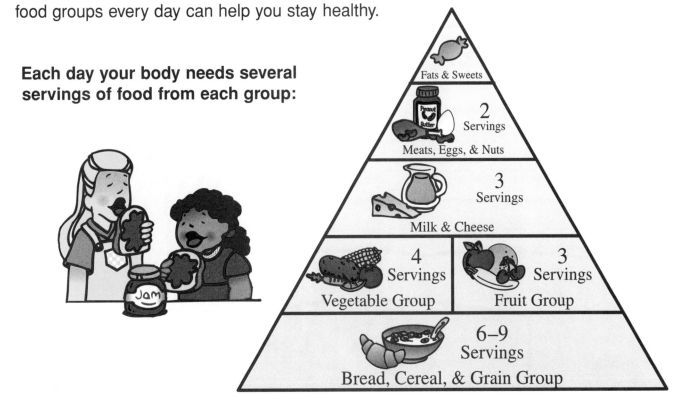

What foods did you eat today?

Which food group did you eat the most foods from today?

From which food group did you eat the least?

Which meal included the most food groups?

Meal Planning

Plan out three balanced meals for one day. Arrange your meals so that by the end of the day, you will have had all the recommended servings of the food groups listed on the Food Pyramid.

Breakfast

_____

_____

_____

_____

_____

Lunch

_____

_____

_____

_____

_____

Dinner

_____

_____

_____

_____

_____

Meal Tracker

Use these charts to record the servings from each food group you eat for one or two weeks. Have another family member keep track, too, and compare.

	Breads / Cereals	Milk	Meat	Fruits	Vegetables	Fats/ Sweets
Monday						
Tuesday						
Wednesday						
Thursday						
Friday						
Saturday						
Sunday						

	Breads / Cereals	Milk	Meat	Fruits	Vegetables	Fats/ Sweets
Monday						
Tuesday						
Wednesday						
Thursday						
Friday						
Saturday						
Sunday						

	Breads / Cereals	Milk	Meat	Fruits	Vegetables	Fats/ Sweets
Monday						
Tuesday						
Wednesday						
Thursday						
Friday						
Saturday						
Sunday						

	Breads / Cereals	Milk	Meat	Fruits	Vegetables	Fats/ Sweets
Monday						
Tuesday						
Wednesday						
Thursday						
Friday						
Saturday						
Sunday						

Get Moving!

Did you know that getting no exercise can be almost as bad for you as smoking?! So get moving this summer!

Summer is the perfect time to get out and get in shape. Your fitness program should include three parts:

- Get 30 minutes of aerobic exercise per day, three to five days a week.

- Exercise your muscles to improve strength and flexibility.

- Make it FUN! Do things that you like to do. Include your friends and family.

Couch Potato Quiz

1. Name three things you do each day that get you moving.

2. Name three things you do a few times a week that are good exercise.

3. How many hours do you spend each week playing outside or exercising?

4. How much TV do you watch each day?

5. How much time do you spend playing computer or video games?

If the time you spend on activities 4 and 5 adds up to more than you spend on 1–3, you could be headed for a spud's life!

Activity Pyramid

The Activity Pyramid works like the Food Pyramid. You can use the Activity Pyramid to help plan your summer exercise program. Fill in the blanks below.

List 1 thing that isn't good exercise that you could do less of this summer.

1._____

Cut Down On

TV time
video or computer games
sitting for more than
30 minutes at a time

List 3 fun activities you enjoy that get you moving and are good exercise.

1._____

2._____

3._____

List 3 exercises you could do to build strength and flexibility this summer.

1._____

2._____

3._____

2–3 Times a Week

Work & Play
bowling
swinging
fishing
jump rope
yard work

Strength & Stretching
dancing
martial arts
gymnastics
push-ups/pull-ups

List 3 activities you would like to do for aerobic exercise this summer.

1._____

2._____

3._____

List 2 sports you would like to participate in this summer.

1._____

2._____

3–5 Times a Week
at least 20 minutes

Aerobic Exercise
walking   skating
running   bicycling
swimming

Sports/Recreation
soccer   relay races
basketball   tennis
volleyball   baseball

Every Day

walk
play outside
take the stairs
bathe your pet

help with chores:
sweeping
washing dishes
picking up
clothes and toys

Adapted from the President's Council on Fitness and Sports

List 5 everyday things you can do to get moving more often.

1._____

2._____

3._____

4._____

5._____

Fitness Fundamentals

Basic physical fitness includes several things:

Cardiovascular Endurance. Your cardiovascular system includes your heart and blood vessels. You need a strong heart to pump your blood. Your blood delivers oxygen and nutrients to your body.

Muscular Strength. This is how strong your muscles are.

Muscular Endurance. Endurance has to do with how long you can use your muscles before they get tired.

Flexibility. This is your ability to move your joints and to use your muscles through their full range of motion.

Body Composition. Your body is made up of what is called lean mass and fat mass.

Lean mass includes the water, muscles, tissues, and organs in your body.

Fat mass includes the fat your body stores for energy. Exercise helps you burn body fat and maintain good body composition.

The goal of a summer fitness program is to improve in all the areas of physical fitness.

You build cardiovascular endurance through **aerobic** exercise. For **aerobic** exercise, you need to work large muscle groups at a steady pace. This increases your heart rate and breathing. You can jog, walk, hike, swim, dance, do aerobics, ride a bike, go rowing, climb stairs, rollerblade, play golf, backpack…

You should get at least 30 minutes of aerobic exercise per day, three to five days a week.

You build muscular strength and endurance with exercises that work your muscles, like sit-ups, push-ups, pull-ups, and weight lifting.

Flexibility. You can increase flexibility through stretching exercises. These are good for warm-ups too.

Find these fitness words.

Word Bank

aerobic	exercise	fat
muscular	flexible	blood
endurance	strength	oxygen
heart rate	joint	hiking

```
u a e y i d t y a g d x p o b
o l s h s t r e n g t h l r c
e w l o o o z v s d m i h d t
g t z w s j o i n t m n k a o
s q a c h i p s a d e t f f m
k c q r x i q f l e x i b l e
e e j o t v k w t e u r g e g
i e s e d r v i n t n f k x o
k e l i d c a d n n e g e j w
u z e d c y u e i g g x i c i
j c i b o r e a h h y w v s i
a m r a a c e m x x x y d i g
f p v n p n d x u s o x e f k
p o c b l o o d e g z a x m c
l e m u s c u l a r m k g i s
```

Your Summer Fitness Program

Start your summer fitness program by choosing at least one aerobic activity from your Activity Pyramid. You can choose more than one for variety.

_____   _____   _____

Do this activity three to five times each week. Keep it up for at least 20 minutes each time.
(Exercise hard enough to increase your heart rate and your breathing. But don't exercise so hard that you get dizzy or can't catch your breath.)

● ●

Use this chart to plan when you will exercise or to record your activity after you exercise.

DATE	ACTIVITY	TIME

DATE	ACTIVITY	TIME

Plan a reward for meeting your exercise goals for two weeks.
(You can make copies of this chart to track your fitness all summer long.)

Start Slow!
Remember to start out slow. Exercise is about getting stronger. It's not about being superman—or superwoman—right off the bat.

Are You Up to the Challenge?

The Presidential Physical Fitness Award Program was designed to help kids get into shape and have fun. To earn the award, you take five fitness tests. These are usually given by teachers at school, but you can train for them this summer.

Remember: Start Slow!

1. Curl-ups. Lie on the floor with your knees bent and your feet about 12 inches from your buttocks. Cross your arms over your chest. Raise your trunk up and touch your elbows to your thighs. Do as many as you can in one minute.

2. Shuttle Run. Draw a starting line. Put two blocks 30 feet away. Run the 30 feet, pick up a block, and bring it back to the starting line. Then run and bring back the second block. Record your fastest time.

3. V-sit Reach. Sit on the floor with your legs straight and your feet 8 to 12 inches apart. Put a ruler between your feet, pointing past your toes. Have a partner hold your legs straight, and keep your toes pointed up. Link your thumbs together and reach forward, palms down, as far as you can along the ruler.

4. One-Mile Walk/Run. On a track or some safe area, run one mile. You can walk as often as you need to. Finish as fast as possible. (Ages six to seven may want to run a quarter mile; ages eight to nine, half a mile.)

5. Pull-ups. Grip a bar with an overhand grip (the backs of your hands toward your face). Have someone lift you up if you need help. Hang with your arms and legs straight. Pull your body up until your chin is over the bar; then let yourself back down. Do as many as you can.

Make a chart to track your progress. Keep working all summer to see if you can improve your score.

If you want to earn the Presidential Physical Fitness Award, you can find information at www.fitness.gov

Respect

Respect is showing good manners toward all people, not just those you know or who are like you. Respect is treating everyone, no matter what religion, race, or culture, male or female, rich or poor, in a way that you would want to be treated.

The easiest way to do this is to decide to **never** take part in activities and to **never** use words that make fun of people because they are different from you or your friends.

It's not necessary for eagles to be crows. What I am, I am.
~ Sitting Bull

Rob, please pass some cake.

Word Find

Find these words that also mean *respect*.

Word Bank	m c e t a r e n e v
honor	w j t a h p s e p t
idolize	e c a d n n t z i w
admire	z v i m w u k i h r
worship	i e c i h b h n s o
recognize	l z e r v b j g r n
appreciate	o i r e k a u o o o
venerate	d r p g m e e c w h
prize	i p p b g c h e r j
	q f a b f g u r r z

Activity

This week go to the library and check out *The Well: David's Story* by Mildred Taylor (1995). The story is set in Mississippi in the early 1900s and tells about David's family, who shares their well with both black and white neighbors. Be sure to read this book with your parents.

Gratitude

Gratitude is when you thank people for the good things they have given you or done for you. Thinking about people and events in your life that make you feel grateful (thankful) will help you become a happier person.

There are over 465 different ways of saying thank you. Here are a few:

Danke   Toda   Merci   Gracias   **Nandri**

Spasibo   Arigato   **Gadda ge**   Paldies   Hvala

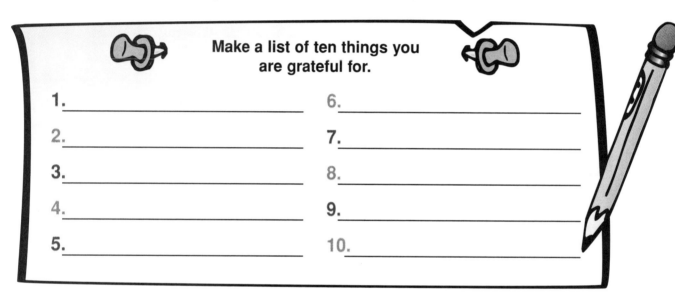

Make a list of ten things you are grateful for.

1. _____   6. _____
2. _____   7. _____
3. _____   8. _____
4. _____   9. _____
5. _____   10. _____

A Recipe for Saying Thanks

1. Make a colorful card.
2. On the inside write a thank-you note to some-one who has done something nice for you.
3. Address an envelope to that person.
4. Pick out a cool stamp.
5. Drop your note in the nearest mailbox.

Saying thank you creates love.

~ Daphne Rose Kingma

Courtesy

If you were the only person in the world, you wouldn't have to have **good manners** or be **courteous**. However, there are over six billion people on our planet, and good manners help us all get along with each other.

Children with good manners are usually well liked by other children and certainly by adults. Here are some simple rules for good manners:

- When you ask for something, say, "Please."
- When someone gives you something, say, "Thank you."
- When someone says, "Thank you," say, "You're welcome."
- If you walk in front of someone or bump into a person, say, "Excuse me."
- When someone else is talking, wait before speaking.
- Share and take turns.

No kindness, no matter how small, is ever wasted. ~ Aesop's Fables

Word Search. Find these words or phrases that deal with *courtesy*.

Word Bank
etiquette
thank you
welcome
excuse me
please
share
turns
patience
polite
manners

```
m u o y k n a h t
e m o c l e w e e
e s a e l p x f c
a m q u f c x r n
e t t e u q i t e
s r g s n r u t i
s r e n n a m g t
v m p o l i t e a
e i e r a h s h p
```

I've Got Manners

Make a colorful poster to display on your bedroom door or on the refrigerator. List five ways you are going to practice your manners. Be creative and decorate with watercolors, poster paints, pictures cut from magazines, clip art, or geometric shapes.

Instead of making a poster, you could make a mobile to hang from your ceiling that shows five different manners to practice.

Consequences

A consequence is what happens after you choose to do something. Some choices lead to good consequences. Other choices lead to bad consequences. An example of this would be choosing whether to eat an apple or a bag of potato chips. The potato chips might seem like a more tasty snack, but eating an apple is better for your body. Or, you may not like to do your homework, but if you choose not to, you won't do well in school, and you may not be able to go out with your friends.

It's hard to look into the future and see how a choice will influence what happens today, tomorrow, or years from now. But whenever we choose to do something, there are consequences that go with our choice. That's why it is important to *think before you choose.*

Remember: The easiest choice does not always lead to the best consequence.

We choose to go to the moon not because it's easy, but because it's hard.
~ John F. Kennedy

Activity

Get a copy of *The Tale of Peter Rabbit* by Beatrix Potter. This simple story is full of choices that lead to bad consequences. Write down three choices Peter made and the consequences that occurred. Who made a good choice, and what was the consequence?

Word Find

Find these words that also mean *consequence.*

Word Bank		
result	outcome	fallout
payoff	effect	reaction
product	aftermath	upshot

b	e	h	p	j	c	p	o	j	q
i	t	h	a	e	l	r	w	r	v
z	u	t	y	f	r	o	s	t	v
g	o	a	o	f	e	d	t	o	m
r	l	m	f	e	a	u	r	h	j
e	l	r	f	c	c	c	e	s	e
s	a	e	b	t	t	t	m	p	g
u	f	t	s	e	i	j	t	u	i
l	e	f	e	m	o	c	t	u	o
t	c	a	i	m	n	o	h	f	d

Friendship

Friends come in all sizes, shapes, and ages: brothers, sisters, parents, neighbors, good teachers, and school and sports friends.

There is a saying, "To have a friend you need to be a friend." Can you think of a day when someone might have tried to get you to say or do unkind things to someone else? Sometimes it takes courage to be a real friend.

Recipe for Friendship

1 cup of always listening to ideas and stories
2 pounds of never talking behind a friend's back
1 pound of no mean teasing
2 cups of always helping a friend who needs help

Take these ingredients and mix completely together. Add laughter, kindness, hugs, and even tears. Bake for as long as it takes to make your friendship good and strong.

I get by with a little help from my friends.

~ John Lennon

Family Night at the Movies

Rent *Toy Story* or *Toy Story II*. Each movie is a simple, yet powerful, tale about true friendship. Fix a big bowl of popcorn to share with your family during the show.

International Friendship Day

The first Sunday in August is International Friendship Day. This is a perfect day to remember all your friends and how they have helped you during your friendship. Give your friends a call or send them an email or snail-mail card.

Confidence

People are **confident**, or have **confidence**, when they feel like they can succeed at a certain task. To feel confident about doing something, most people need to practice a task over and over.

Reading, pitching a baseball, writing in cursive, playing the flute, even mopping a floor are all examples of tasks that need to be practiced before people feel confident they can succeed.

What are five things you feel confident doing?

What is one thing you want to feel more confident doing?

Make a plan for how and when you will practice until you feel confident.

You Crack Me Up!

Materials needed:
1 dozen eggs
a mixing bowl

Cracking eggs without breaking the yolk or getting egg whites all over your hands takes practice.

1. Watch an adult break an egg into the bowl. How did they hold their hands? How did they pull the egg apart?

2. Now you try. Did you do a perfect job the first time? Keep trying until you begin to feel confident about cracking eggs.

3. Use the eggs immediately to make a cheese omelet or custard pie. Refrigerate any unused eggs for up to three days.

Pride

Never bend your head.

Always hold it high.

Look the world

Right in the eye.

~ Helen Keller

Responsibility

You show **responsibility** by doing what you agree or promise to do. It might be a task, such as a homework assignment, or a chore, such as feeding your gerbil.

When you are young, your parents and teachers will give you simple tasks like putting away toys or brushing your teeth without being asked. As you get older, you will be given more responsibility. You might be trusted to come home from a friend's house at a certain time or drive to the store for groceries.

It takes a lot of practice to grow up to be a responsible person. The easiest way to practice is by keeping your promises and doing what you know is right.

A parent is responsible for different things than a child or a teenager. Write three activities you are responsible for every day. Then write three things a parent is responsible for every day.

If you want your eggs hatched, sit on them yourself. ~ Haitian Proverb

Activity

Materials needed:
21 pennies or counters such as beans, rocks, or marbles
2 small containers labeled #1 and #2

Decide on a reward for successfully completing this activity.
Put all the counters in container #1.
Review the three activities you are responsible for every day.
Each night before you go to bed, put one counter for each completed activity into container #2. At the end of seven days count all the counters in container #2.

If you have 16 or more counters in container #2, you are on your way to becoming very responsible. Collect your reward.
My reward is_____.

Service/Helping

Service is **helping** another person or group of people without asking for any kind of reward or payment. These are some good things that happen when you do service:

1. You feel closer to the people in your community (neighborhood).
2. You feel pride in yourself when you see that you can help other people in need.
3. Your family feels proud of you.
4. You will make new friends as you help others.

An old saying goes, "Charity begins at home." This means that you don't have to do big, important-sounding things to help people. You can start in your own home and neighborhood.

Activity

Each day this week, do one act of service around your house. Don't ask for or take any kind of payment or reward. Be creative! Possible acts of service are:

1. Carry in the groceries, do the dishes, or fold the laundry.
2. Read aloud to a younger brother or sister.
3. Make breakfast or pack lunches.
4. Recycle newspapers and cans.
5. Clean the refrigerator or your room.

At the end of the week, think of a project to do with your family that will help your community. You could play musical instruments or sing at a nursing home, set up a lemonade stand and give the money you make to the Special Olympics, offer to play board games with children in the hospital, or pick some flowers and take them to a neighbor. The list goes on and on.

> **All the flowers of tomorrow are in the seeds of today.**
> ~ **Indian Proverb**

Word Find

Find these words that also mean *service*.

Word Bank

help	assist	aid
charity	support	boost
benefit	contribute	guide

```
m v l a o d w f d r
c o n t r i b u t e
t b s x c a z v x q
s g p q g w b n y t
i v l y g u v x z i
s n e t e x m n m f
s f h d u d g t e e
a u c h a r i t y n
s u p p o r t u x e
b o o s t g f j g b
```

Honesty and Trust

Being an **honest** person means you don't steal, cheat, or tell lies. **Trust** is when you believe someone will be honest. If you are dishonest, or not truthful, people will not trust you.

You want to tell the truth because it is important to have your family and friends trust you. However, it takes courage to tell the truth, especially if you don't want people to get mad at you or be disappointed in the way you behaved.

How would your parents feel if you lied to them? People almost always find out about lies, and most parents will be more angry about a lie than if you had told them the truth in the first place.

When family or friends ask about something, remember that honesty is telling the truth. Honesty is telling what really happened. Honesty is keeping your promises. *Be proud of being an honest person.*

Write down five feeling words about how you felt when you *weren't* honest or trusted.	Write down five feeling words about how you felt when you *were* honest or trusted.
1._____	1._____
2._____	2._____
3._____	3._____
4._____	4._____
5._____	5._____

Parent note: Help your child by pointing out times he or she acted honestly.

Count to Ten

Tape ten pieces of colored paper to your refrigerator. For one week, each time you tell the truth or keep a promise, take one piece of paper down and put it in the recycling bin. If all ten pieces of paper are gone by the end of the week, collect your reward.

Honesty is the first chapter in the book of wisdom.
~ Thomas Jefferson

My reward is_____.

Happiness

Happiness is a feeling that comes when you enjoy your life. Different things make different people happy. Some people feel happy when they are playing soccer. Other people feel happy when they are playing the cello. It is important to understand what makes you happy so you can include some of these things in your daily plan.

These are some actions that show you are happy: laughing, giggling, skipping, smiling, and hugging.

Make a list of seven activities that make you feel happy.

1._____

2._____

3._____

4._____

5._____

6._____

7._____

Bonus!

List two things you could do to make someone else happy.

1._____

2._____

Activity

Write down a plan to do one activity each day this week that makes you happy.

Try simple things—listen to your favorite song, play with a friend, bake muffins, shoot hoops, etc.

Be sure to thank everyone who helps you and don't forget to laugh!

Happy Thought

The world is so full

of a number of things,

I'm sure we should

all be happy as kings.

~Robert Louis Stevenson

Notes

Five things I'm thankful for:

1. _____
2. _____
3. _____
4. _____
5. _____

Notes

Five things I'm thankful for:

1. _____
2. _____
3. _____
4. _____
5. _____